CLASSICS IN EDUCATION
Lawrence A. Cremin, General Editor

☆ ☆ ☆

THE REPUBLIC AND THE SCHOOL
Horace Mann on the Education of Free Men
Edited by Lawrence A. Cremin

AMERICAN IDEAS ABOUT ADULT EDUCATION
1710–1951
Edited by C. Hartley Grattan

DEWEY ON EDUCATION
Introduction and Notes by Martin S. Dworkin

THE SUPREME COURT AND EDUCATION
Edited by David Fellman

INTERNATIONAL EDUCATION
A Documentary History
Edited by David G. Scanlon

CRUSADE AGAINST IGNORANCE
Thomas Jefferson on Education
Edited by Gordon C. Lee

CHINESE EDUCATION UNDER COMMUNISM
Edited by Chang-tu Hu

CHARLES W. ELIOT AND POPULAR EDUCATION
Edited by Edward A. Krug

WILLIAM T. HARRIS ON EDUCATION
(in preparation)
Edited by Martin S. Dworkin

THE *EMILE* OF JEAN JACQUES ROUSSEAU
Selections
Translated and Edited by William Boyd

THE MINOR EDUCATIONAL WRITINGS OF
JEAN JACQUES ROUSSEAU
Selected and Translated by William Boyd

PSYCHOLOGY AND THE SCIENCE OF EDUCATION
Selected Writings of Edward L. Thorndike
Edited by Geraldine M. Joncich

THE NEW-ENGLAND PRIMER
Introduction by Paul Leicester Ford

BENJAMIN FRANKLIN ON EDUCATION
Edited by John Hardin Best

THE COLLEGES AND THE PUBLIC
1787–1862
Edited by Theodore Rawson Crane

TRADITIONS OF AFRICAN EDUCATION
Edited by David G. Scanlon

NOAH WEBSTER'S AMERICAN SPELLING BOOK
Introductory Essay by Henry Steele Commager

EMERSON ON EDUCATION
Selections
Edited by Howard Mumford Jones

ECONOMIC INFLUENCES UPON EDUCATIONAL
PROGRESS IN THE UNITED STATES, 1820–1850
By Frank Tracy Carlton
Foreword by Lawrence A. Cremin

QUINTILIAN ON EDUCATION
Selected and Translated by William M. Smail

ROMAN EDUCATION FROM CICERO
TO QUINTILIAN
By Aubrey Gwynn, S.J.

HERBERT SPENCER ON EDUCATION
Edited by Andreas M. Kazamias

JOHN LOCKE'S *OF THE CONDUCT
OF THE UNDERSTANDING*
Edited by Francis W. Garforth

Herbert Spencer
on Education

Edited, with an Introduction and Notes, by

ANDREAS M. KAZAMIAS

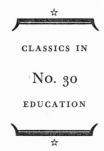

CLASSICS IN

No. 30

EDUCATION

TEACHERS COLLEGE PRESS
TEACHERS COLLEGE, COLUMBIA UNIVERSITY
NEW YORK

Foreword

Herbert Spencer's influence on American education has been widely recognized and amply documented. The four essays that constituted his *Education: Intellectual, Moral, and Physical* (1860) were probably the most frequently read of all his publications on both sides of the Atlantic, and their uncompromising insistence on science as the essence of a modern curriculum found ready acceptance among those seeking to reform American schools and colleges. Beyond this, the more general treatises that eventually composed his *Synthetic Philosophy* profoundly shaped the ways in which scholars came to conceive of education and its role in society. As Richard Hofstadter has observed, it was virtually impossible to be involved in any area of intellectual activity at the end of the nineteenth century without somehow coming to terms with Spencer; and the resultant impact of his ideas on psychology, sociology, and ethics—to name but three fields—was bound ultimately to affect education.

Yet granting this, the precise nature of Spencer's influence has never been fully determined. Ideas are always transmitted selectively, and the processes by which one society borrows and uses the ideas of another are subtle, complicated, and often confusing. Thus, for example, we know full well that William Graham Sumner's doubts about the power of popular schooling derived from his study of Spencer; but then, so did Lester Frank Ward's enthusiasm for the extension of educational opportunity. Similarly, we know that Spencer strengthened the utili-

tarian tendencies of early twentieth-century educational
reform in the United States; and yet there is no denying
that the narrow utilitarianism of a report such as *Cardinal Principles of Secondary Education* (1918) went far
beyond anything Spencer ever espoused. To what extent
is a thinker responsible for the uses and effects of his ideas?

To unravel these threads of influence, to separate what
Spencer actually said from what his disciples and critics
inferred, wrote, and did, is a problem that needs much
fuller exploration if we are to understand the development of American educational theory and practice over
the past hundred years. For, as Professor Kazamias points
out, Spencer has become part of our "conventional educational wisdom," the sources of which are too little
understood. And it is only as we go back to those sources
that we can gain the critical perspective required for
thoughtful educational advance.

LAWRENCE A. CREMIN

Contents

Herbert Spencer: Prophet of Individualism and Scientific Culture

By ANDREAS M. KAZAMIAS

To many Englishmen the death of Queen Victoria in 1901 signified the demise of a glorious era and signalled the dawn of a new social and moral order. By that time much of what they associated with Victorianism in politics, economics, religion, education, and morals was assessed as more or less a casualty of history, and few were prepared to shed any tears over its passing. Recently, however, and conspicuously during the period following the Second World War, there has been a renewed interest in the Victorian era. Apart from a tinge of the romanticism that so often seems to characterize "returns to the past," the return to the Victorians has also been marked by serious scholarly dives into what now emerges as a vast, turbulent, and often inscrutable world. We now have not only comprehensive histories of the period, covering the gamut of events and ideas, but also innumerable monographs and biographical studies on a great many facets of Victorian life and thought. Yet, there are conspicuous lacunae, even in the case of some of the most notable Victorians. Such indeed is the case with Herbert Spencer, who, more than any of his contemporaries, epitomized some of the most distinctive features of the Victorian frame of mind. It is the purpose of this small volume to present a profile of Spencer's ideas, particularly those pertaining to education, which reflect some of his general views about the individual and society and which contributed immeasurably to his great popularity at home and abroad.

AN EARNEST AND EMINENT VICTORIAN

The landscape at which Spencer had gazed as a boy and whose natural treasures he had sought to explore changed drastically during his long lifetime (1820–1903), a common occurrence in nineteenth century England. Spencer, writing in the closing decades of the century,[1] recalled that during his boyhood Number 12 Exeter Row, Derby, was a new house "forming one member of a street partially built on one side only; and its small garden was separated by a meadow from the river Derwent, on the other side of which lay the mass of the town." But about sixty years later the house had become "decayed and dingy," having been "swallowed up by increasing suburbs and enveloped in the smoke of factories and foundries."[2] The face of England had changed, perhaps

[1] For biographical information on Spencer, the most valuable source continues to be his own testament, published posthumously, *An Autobiography* (2 vols.; New York: D. Appleton and Co., 1904), cited hereafter as *Autobiography*. Another valuable source is Spencer's only biography, by David Duncan, who for about three years served as Spencer's secretary and helper: *Life and Letters of Herbert Spencer* (2 vols.; New York: D. Appleton and Co., 1908), cited hereafter as *Life and Letters*. Two other character portraits by people who knew Spencer intimately are equally revealing. One of these is by Beatrice (Potter) Webb, wife of Sidney Webb and a key figure in the Fabian socialist movement: *My Apprenticeship* (New York: Longmans, Green and Co., 1926), pp. 21–38. The other sketch is by James Collier, who served as Spencer's secretary and amanuensis, in Josiah Royce's *Herbert Spencer: An Estimate and Review* (New York: Fox, Duffield and Co., 1904), pp. 187–234.

[2] *Autobiography*, I, 71.

partly as a result of the evolutionary law of change, from the homogeneous and simple to the heterogeneous and complex; but, according to Spencer, certain of his own ancestral traits remained constant throughout his life.

Spencer was born and reared in a middle class family of the type which, during the early decades of the nineteenth century, manifested some of the most salient features of English Philistinism, with its "hedgehog-like independence, its remorseless energy, its contempt for the pleasures and graces of life."[3] Spencer himself attributed many of what he felt were distinctive features of his personality and views to his Nonconformist, individualistic, rebellious, and "puritan" background. "Has there not been inheritance of these ancestral traits, or some of them?" he asked. "That the spirit of non-conformity," he wrote on one occasion, "is shown by me in various directions, no one can deny: the disregard of authority, political, religious, or social, is very conspicuous."[4]

Of all the ancestral traits, Spencer and those who knew him often singled out heterodoxy, aversion to authority, and an uncompromising aggressive individualism as distinctive of what has been referred to as "the phenomenon of Spencer." In all "practical affairs"—political, economic, educational, and moral—he remained to the end, a passionate devotee of individual liberty and nonconformity. Spencer was a vitriolic critic by word and deed of any type of regulatory activity—be it in the nature of governmental interference or parental authority, of religious orthodoxy or conventional morality—which would threaten to stifle or curtail the "natural

[3] Esmé Wingfield-Stratford, *Those Earnest Victorians* (London: William Morrow and Co., 1930), p. 251.

[4] *Autobiography*, I, 13. Also see pp. 170–171, where he attributes his own "repugnance" to ecclesiasticism and "priestly rule" to the influence of his father's views.

rights" of the individual (adult or child) or to constrain his natural development. The only types of authority to which he would willingly pay homage and respect were universal "principles" of human existence and a "Divine impersonal authority."[5] Spencer's testimony, as well as the accounts of many who knew him, is replete with episodes illustrating such characteristics.

In matters of political belief or affiliation he referred to himself as "radical," or in sympathy with the Liberals, especially the early Gladstonian Liberals, when forced to choose between the two major political parties (Liberals and Tories). But, more often than not, he dissented from the views of both major political groups, especially "on the question of the functions of the State." Later in his life, he was quite indifferent to active political participation because, as he put it, ". . . [as] Liberals have vied with Conservatives in extending legislative regulations in all directions, there has been nothing to choose between them, and therefore, no temptation to vote."[6] Most revealing, perhaps, of his fealty to those "principles" of which his biographer spoke were Spencer's recollections of his reaction to the famous Reform Bill of 1867. At

[5] *Life and Letters,* II, 247.

[6] *Autobiography,* II, 146. Spencer cast his vote only once (in the election of 1865). Twenty years later, when asked to allow his name to be entered as a candidate for Parliament from Leicester, he declined in typical Spencerian fashion. Aside from reasons of health and his belief that the influence which a member of Parliament possessed was overestimated anyway, he felt that if chosen he would "prove a very impracticable member." His views on political matters, he wrote to the Reverend J. Page Hopps in 1884, "are widely divergent from those of all political parties at present existing." This, he continued, would place him "in continual antagonism with my constituents," for they would expect him to vote for measures of which he disapproved. The upshot of such disagreement would be that he would be quickly "called upon to resign." (*Life and Letters,* I, 319–321.)

first, Spencer reminisced, he gladly approved of the measure because of "the seemingly-just principle of giving equal political powers to all men."[7] Yet, upon calmer reflection, he saw that it was his feeling rather than his intellect that guided him in his hasty reaction. Had he reasoned deductively or from a priori principles, as he often did, he would have arrived at the same conclusion as had become clear a posteriori fifteen years after the passing of the 1867 act. Spencer's own words in this connection not only reveal the mode of much of his thinking, but they also indicate certain of his assumptions concerning social class political behavior:

I might have inferred *a priori,* that which has now become clear *a posteriori,* that the change would result in replacing the old class-legislation by a new class-legislation. It is certain that, given the average human nature now existing, those who have power will pursue, indirectly if not directly, obscurely if not clearly, their own interests, or rather their apparent interests. We have no reason for supposing that the lower classes are intrinsically better than the higher classes. Hence if, while the last were predominant, they made laws which in one way or other favoured themselves, it follows that now, when the first are predominant, they also will give legislation a bias to their own advantage. Manifest as it always was, it has now become more manifest still, that, so long as governmental action is unrestricted, the thing required is a representation of *interests;* and that a system under which one interest is overwhelmingly represented (whether it be that of a smaller or of a larger section of the community) will issue in one-sided laws.[8]

One might readily refute such categorical statements either on the grounds of historical accuracy (there was no dominance of the lower classes in England at the time

---

[7] Actually the Reform Bill of 1867 did not extend the franchise "to all men," but only to the urban working classes. The agricultural working man was still denied the parliamentary vote.

[8] *Autobiography,* II, 433.

he was writing, in 1882) or on the grounds that he assumed a necessary incompatibility or conflict of class-in-
terests. Nevertheless, for the Marxist or the proponent of
the welfare state, Spencer raises an important problem,
namely the persistent danger to individual freedom of
any dominant bureaucracy, be it aristocratic, democratic,
or socialistic.

In the religious domain Spencer was heterodox and
agnostic. He tells us that he was "averse to ecclesiasticism," that "the creed of Christendom" was "alien" to
his "nature," and that religious worship yielded no
"pleasure."[9] In his heterodoxy and agnosticism Spencer
did not stand alone. Victorian religion was as marked by
momentous crises, rifts, and challenges as it was by
orthodoxy. Apart from internal dissensions (differences
between high, low, and broad Anglicanism, the Oxford
Movement, the growth of Nonconformity and Cathol-
icism), Victorian religion faced its greatest challenges
from the development of science and from a naturalistic
and evolutionary interpretation of morality. In the mid-
decades of the century, particularly in the 1860's, traditional Victorian beliefs about man, life, and religion
received their most shocking jolt. This was in large part
due to the doctrine of evolution, the biological aspects of
which were examined scientifically in the famous paper
by Darwin and Wallace before the Linnaean Society
(1858) and in Darwin's monumental *The Origin of Species* (1859). The theory of evolution in some form, however, had been entertained by scientists and philosophers
before Darwin. Spencer, in particular, had already published two articles, "The Development Hypothesis"
(1852) and "Progress: Its Law and Cause" (1857), and in
fact had coined the phrase "survival of the fittest," which

9 *Ibid*, I, 171.

came to be associated with the evolutionary doctrine.[10] But Spencer generalized Darwin's theory to encompass all phenomena (organic, inorganic, and superorganic), including society and man's place in it.[11] What is pertinent here is the fact that evolution and, in particular, social evolution, of which Spencer became a leading exponent and publicist, contradicted contemporary religious beliefs about creation and morality.[12] To orthodox theologians an evolutionary view of man and society was irreligious, amoral, and even immoral. Yet the religious agnosticism of Spencer, as indeed that of other eminent Victorians, was accompanied by a strong moral "puritanism."[13] Perhaps this partly accounts for some "oddities"

[10] *Ibid.*, pp. 448–449. Spencer in fact tells us that his belief in the "progressive modifications" of organic forms "physically caused and inherited" went back to his boyhood years (*ibid.*, p. 201).

[11] See Spencer's essay "Progress: Its Law and Cause," first published in the *Westminster Review* (April, 1857). In it Spencer wrote that the "law of organic progress is the law of all progress" in the development of the earth, society, government, language, literature, science, art, etc. (Spencer, *Essays on Education, Etc.* [London: J. M. Dent and Sons Ltd., 1911], p. 154; cited hereafter as *Essays, Etc*). A letter to Spencer by Darwin, dated November 25, 1858, is particularly interesting. In it Darwin wrote: "Your remarks on the general argument of the so-called Development Theory seem to me admirable. I am at present preparing an abstract of a larger work on the changes of species; but I treat the subject simply as a naturalist, and not from the general point of view; otherwise, in my opinion, your argument could not have been improved on, and might have been quoted by me with great advantage." (*Life and Letters*, I, 113.)

[12] The famous encounter between Samuel Wilberforce, Bishop of Oxford, and T. H. Huxley at the annual meeting of the British Association for the Advancement of Science in 1860 is a telling example of the conflict between orthodox theologians and the new scientific spirit. See Cyril Bibby, *T. H. Huxley: Scientist, Humanist and Educator* (London: C. A. Watts and Co. Ltd., 1959), pp. 69–70. Also see Thomas H. Huxley, *Man's Place in Nature* (Ann Arbor: University of Michigan Press, 1959), pp. 2–3.

[13] On the moral "puritanism" of the Victorian agnostics, see

in his character and the earnestness of his pursuits. In this connection one is often reminded of Spencer's uncomfortable relations with the opposite sex (according to James Collier, his secretary and amanuensis, even his admiration for George Eliot "was due probably to the fact that he never regarded the great novelist as a normal woman");[14] or of the incident on a fishing expedition at Beoch when Spencer got his line tangled and for the first and only time in his life "vented an oath."[15] "Poor Spencer," his friend Mr. Potter once said to his daughter Beatrice (Mrs. Webb), "he lacks instinct, my dear, he lacks instinct—you will discover that instinct is as important as intellect."[16]

It is significant to point out that, in spite of his obvious hostility toward certain aspects of Victorian religion and his faith in a scientific, evolutionary explanation of existence and morality, Spencer, like many of his contempo-

---

G. D. Klingopoulos, "Notes on the Victorian Scene," in Boris Ford, ed., *From Dickens to Hardy* (Hammondsworth, Middlesex: Penguin Books Ltd., 1958), pp. 54–56.

[14] Royce, *op. cit.*, p. 225. Another illustrative episode is recounted by Spencer himself. Some friends of his had taken upon themselves to find him a wife. A certain Miss Evans was highly impressed by *Social Statics*, Spencer's first book, which appeared when he was thirty years old, and his friends arranged a meeting of the author and the possible bride. Spencer wrote after the meeting: "So that though she is sufficiently good-looking, young, extremely open, a poetess and an heiress, I do not think that the spirit will move me" (*Autobiography*, I, 422–423).

[15] About this incident, Spencer, who at the time was thirty-six years old, wrote: "I suppose it was the oddity of this incident which drew my attention to the fact that, being then thirty-six years of age, I had never before been betrayed into intemperate speech of such kind" (*Autobiography*, I, 570).

[16] Webb, *op. cit.*, p. 24. Another acquaintance described Spencer as "all head and no heart" (F. J. C. Hearnshaw, ed., *The Social and Political Ideas of Some Representative Thinkers of the Victorian Age* [New York: Barnes and Noble, 1930], p. 55).

raries, was neither amoral nor irreligious, if by these labels one means the absence of an intense earnestness about the mysteries of man and the universe.[17] Although clearly a devotee of scientific truth, he also believed that "positive knowledge does not, and never can, fill the whole region of possible thought." In the first part of his *First Principles* Spencer sought to bring about a "reconciliation" between science and religion by maintaining that they represent two modes of thought developing out of the "progress of intelligence," one concerned with the "natural" and the other with the "supernatural." Yet both science and religion are parts of "the whole," which is "Absolute," "Inscrutable," or "Unknowable."[18]

It was quite characteristic of many of the Victorian "scientists" or proponents of science, including Spencer, to wrestle with the relationship between science and religion. Although science had opened up new vistas of the world, the universe, man, and his institutions and was thus heralded with much optimism and self-assurance, there also seemed to be an uneasiness about ignoring religion. At times Spencer went to great pains to provide a religious justification for science. In his famous educational essay "What Knowledge Is of Most Worth?" Spencer devoted considerable space to a discussion of the relation-

[17] Duncan, his biographer, wrote: "The mysteries of existence remained mysteries to the last. Though he did not accept the dogmas of any creed, he was in the truest sense, religious. 'In private life,' says Mr. Troughton, 'he refrained from obtruding his heterodox views upon others, nor have I ever known him give utterance to any language which could possibly be construed as scoffing. . . . The name of the Founder of Christianity always elicited his profound respect.' Mr. Troughton recalls more than one occasion on which Spencer strongly condemned language which appeared irreverent." (*Life and Letters*, II, 249–250.)

[18] Spencer, *First Principles of a New System of Philosophy* (2nd ed.; New York: D. Appleton and Co., 1868), Part I.

ship between scientific education or "culture" and religious "culture," as well as to the significance of the study of science for "moral discipline." He agreed with T. H. Huxley, his agnostic scientist friend, who said that "true science and true religion are twin sisters, and the separation of either from the other is sure to prove the death of both." To Spencer "true science," which delved into "the profound" rather than the superficial, cultivated a sort of spiritual orientation better than the traditional "humanistic" studies. In his own words: "It generates a profound respect for, and an implicit faith in, those uniformities of action which all things disclose," and it alone "can give us the true conception of ourselves and our relation to the mysteries of existence."[19]

In education, Spencer found yet another arena in which to assert his aversion to authority and his defense of individual liberty. Spencer's educational ideas are discussed more fully later; here we will merely mention a few points which illustrate further the temperament of the man, his intellectual proclivities, and the Victorian context. Always inclined to stress his own originality, Spencer refused W. H. Hudson permission to dedicate a book on Rousseau to him, primarily because he rejected the implications made on several occasions that he had borrowed many of his political and educational views from the French writer.[20] Emphasizing the "natural

[19] *Essays, Etc.*, pp. 40–42. Also see other statements on the moral significance of science in *Education: Intellectual, Moral, and Physical* (London: G. Manwaring, 1861), pp. 52, 113–115, 125–126.

[20] The main reference in his letter to W. H. Hudson, written only a few months before Spencer's death, was a statement made by Huxley in a letter to the *London Times* some years earlier that Spencer had adopted some of his political views on equality from Rousseau. But clearly Spencer had in mind other references, particularly to the fact that Gabriel Compayré, the French educational historian, had called Spencer a "genuine disciple of the author of

rights of children," he was averse to "undesirable submissiveness" and to undue parental authority. Beatrice Webb recalled, "To the children of the household the philosopher always appeared in the guise of a liberator." Spencer's criticisms of contemporary disciplinary practices infuriated Beatrice's mother, her governess, and the "old fashioned dame" in charge of the local school. On one occasion, Mrs. Webb noted, the governess said to her pupils: "You can go out this morning, my dears, with Mr. Spencer, and mind you follow his teaching and do exactly what you have a mind to."[21] In other educational matters as well Spencer appeared "in the guise of a liberator." He shunned the prevalent curriculum of formal schooling because it encouraged "*submissive receptivity* instead of *independent activity*";[22] he considered it artificial, dogmatic, constraining for intellectual development, and based on authority.[23]

Fortunately, he felt, his own education and intellectual training had been free from superficialities and dogmatism. His mind had been allowed to feed on "natural culture" and to explore with originality the phenomena of nature, society, and man. His own educational back-

---

Émile." According to Duncan, Spencer "had been at pains to point out to Mr. Gabriel Compayré in October, 1901, that he had never read *Émile,* and owed none of his ideas on education to it" (*Life and Letters,* II, 212–213). Actually, although Spencer did not read Rousseau, he was acquainted with the Frenchman's educational views on discipline through Rousseau's followers in England. But it should also be stated that many of Spencer's educational ideas were based on sheer common sense or were in line with his overall conceptual scheme of natural development and freedom from any kinds of constraints. See R. L. Archer, *Secondary Education in the Nineteenth Century* (Cambridge, England: The University Press, 1932), pp. 121–123.

21 Webb, *op. cit.,* p. 25.
22 *Autobiography,* I, 388.
23 *Life and Letters,* II, 306.

ground seemed to provide adequate justification for broader generalizations, and, he reasoned:

The very conception of training, as carried on in the past and as still carried on, implies forcing of the mind into shapes it would not otherwise have taken—implies a bending of the shoots out of their lines of spontaneous growth into conformity with a pattern. Evidently, then, a mind trained, in the ordinary sense of the word, loses some of its innate potentialities.[24]

Reference to Spencer's dissent in education cannot, of course, be restricted to pedagogical matters such as curriculum and discipline; pedagogical practices, according to him, were integral parts of "modes of culture" which were themselves interrelated with other social institutions (religious, political, economic, etc.). Therefore Spencer's advocacy of pedagogical liberalism and absence of restraint was consistent with his advocacy of liberalism and individual freedom in general, which was itself consistent with his social evolutionism. Hence, he also objected to undue state interference and regulation in the practical affairs of life. In this connection Spencer has often been viewed as an extreme exponent of the laissez-faire doctrine in educational policy, a point to which we shall return later.

That Spencer was earnest in his personal and intellectual activities few would deny; so much so in fact that, like other eminent Victorians, he must at times have been a "redoubtable bore."[25] In spite of his exag-

[24] *Autobiography,* I, 386.

[25] See Wingfield-Stratford, *op. cit.,* p. 147. At least one of his closest friends, Mr. Potter, certainly found him so. Mrs. Webb records that her father, in spite of travelling and fishing with Spencer, was bored "past endurance" with "synthetic philosophy" and often remarked, "words, my dear, mere words" (Webb, *op. cit.,* pp. 23–24). Spencer's habit of doubting, arguing, and criticizing rubbed some of his best friends the wrong way and did not con-

gerated views, Spencer was a man of his time. He was certainly in the mainstream of what G. M. Young has described as "the liberal mind in Victorian England." At least this would be true of the liberal mind of the mid-Victorian period, viz., the belief in progress through science or "natural philosophy," as it was often called; "a detestation of all authority, from empires to trade unions"; the belief that self-government was better than good government; and a dynamic rather than a static view of society.[26] Spencer, according to Wingfield-Stratford, was one of the two "great apostles of Victorian individuality" (the other being John Stuart Mill); he articulated in his writings and in his life, perhaps to the "point of caricature," the average Englishman's strong "sentiment of individual liberty."

His [Spencer's] philosophy is long out of date, except for its muscular and downright style, but he only lacks a Boswell to become as representative a figure of the nineteenth, as Dr. Johnson was of the eighteenth century.[27]

Still another well-known student of the Victorian scene,

---

tribute to particularly amicable relationships, let alone to other more romantic attachments. See Royce, *op. cit.,* pp. 224–225. "He is a queer fellow; he's always finding fault with something or other," Spencer recollected, "was the kind of remark made in my presence" (*Autobiography,* I, 162). Yet, it should be remembered, Spencer counted some of the most eminent men of his time as his friends. Aside from T. H. Huxley, there were J. S. Mill, George Eliot, Tyndall, and Hooker. And Mrs. Webb maintained a warm affection for the "professional doubter." Spencer was probably right when he introspected: "Of course the traits of character thus illustrated did not conduce to friendship with those around. After a time, however, the unfavourable impressions at first produced wore off. It was discovered that within the prickly husk the kernel was not quite so harsh as was supposed." (*Ibid.,* p. 163.)

26 G. M. Young, *Victorian Essays* (London: Oxford University Press, 1962), pp. 110–116.

27 Wingfield-Stratford, *op. cit.,* p. 250. Also see pp. 246, 249, 251–254.

Asa Briggs, although not mentioning Spencer, would certainly have included him among those who epitomized the temper of the mid-Victorian decades. In his *Victorian People* Briggs described the period from 1851 to 1867 as follows:

> . . . from its social balance it produced a distinctive civilization of its own. The key words of the times were "thought," "work," and "progress." Clear thinking was preferable to impulse or prejudice and the battle of ideas to the dictatorship of slogans; hard work was considered the foundation of all material advancement; and both clear thinking and hard work were deemed essential to continued national progress.[28]

"Hard work!" Who but a Victorian would engage in such a formidable and vast undertaking as the *Synthetic Philosophy*? Spencer himself was somewhat apologetic "for venturing to deal with so vast and so difficult a subject" as a general theory of evolution which would cover "all orders of existences."[29] Yet, like so many other of the Victorians (Ruskin, Carlyle, Macaulay, and Buckle, to name but a few), he did not demur from embarking upon a gigantic lifetime enterprise. Indeed, if one accepts G. M. Young's view that the Victorian age "is the insular phase of a movement common to the whole of western Europe and its offshoots beyond the seas,"[30] Spencer's brave plunge into speculating about the cosmos as a whole is another manifestation of a tendency common to eighteenth and nineteenth century western thinkers.[31]

---

[28] Asa Briggs, *Victorian People: A Reassessment of Persons and Themes 1851-67* (New York: Harper and Row, 1963), p. 1. First published and copyrighted by the University of Chicago Press, 1955.

[29] *Autobiography*, II, 118–119. William James called Spencer the "philosopher of vastness." For more details on the Victorian propensity toward vast undertakings, and "hard work," also see Wingfield-Stratford, *op. cit.*, pp. 143–144.

[30] Young, *op. cit.*, pp. 110–111.

[31] For a good profile of the writings and ideas of representative thinkers, e.g., Kant, Hegel, Fichte, Comte, Marx, etc., who have

In short, the total range of Spencer's mind and life, however extreme, exaggerated, and eccentric, is part of that complex cluster of ideas, events, and individuals that make up Victorianism and the Victorian Age. Yet, although he shared the Victorian frame of mind, Spencer's ideas are not necessarily circumscribed by the limits of a clearly defined historical period, for the Victorians grappled with questions of universal import: man's place in life, his institutions, and his moral and intellectual development. Some of their answers may not be of great interest today; some we might consider as passé, or even naive; but some of the issues they debated with such fervor and seriousness are quite as relevant for us today as they were in the nineteenth century. Spencer wrestled with such universal issues, and his answers were much in vogue during his lifetime; subsequently, however, his ideas ceased to evoke much interest. In a later section we shall attempt to refute the allegation that the study of Spencer is justifiable only on purely historical grounds, that is only as it sheds light on nineteenth century life and thought.

THE UNSCHOOLED MODERN ARISTOTLE[32]

When one examines Victorian education, one is often intrigued by certain peculiarities or paradoxes, such as the

grappled with such grand designs, see Henry D. Aiken, ed., *The Age of Ideology* (New York: Mentor Books, 1956). Aiken includes Spencer and provides one of the most perceptive recent interpretations of his general philosophy of evolution, pp. 161–170.

[32] Because of his stand against "over legislation" and government regulation, as well as because of the catholicity of his interests and productivity (in psychology, sociology, politics, philosophy, education, etc.), Spencer was hailed as "our modern Aristotle" by the Liberty and Property Defence League. See Herman Ausubel, *The Late Victorians: A Short History* (New York: D. Van Nostrand Co., 1955), pp. 41–46.

fact that some of the most eminent Victorian intellectuals had a bare minimum, if any, of what today is called "formal schooling." The most celebrated Victorian case of a peculiar type of education is that of John Stuart Mill. But the education of Herbert Spencer is equally "strange." To the historian of educational ideas it acquires added relevance for at least two reasons: it sheds light upon the influences on Spencer's intellectual development, and it furnishes additional background for an understanding of Spencer's own views about education.

Spencer would have rejected much of Mill's early education as "ornamental," contrary to the natural development of the child and to the laws of evolution, lopsided, and downright inhumane, for it consisted almost exclusively of classical-humanistic subject matter, and it was bookish and authoritarian. Mill, as far as he could remember, started learning Greek at the age of three, and Latin at eight. Under the close surveillance of his father, by the time he was twelve years old he had read thoroughly most of the ancient classics, elementary geometry and algebra, differential calculus, and other portions of the "higher mathematics." At twelve he began with Aristotle's *Organon,* and then proceeded to Hobbes' *Computatio Sive Logica.* And at thirteen his father took him "through a complete course in political economy" (Ricardo, Adam Smith, etc.).[33]

Consider now the education of Herbert Spencer during the same age period. Where Mill's was incredibly abundant, Spencer's was deplorably lacking:

I knew nothing worth mentioning of Latin or Greek. . . . Moreover I was wholly uninstructed in English—using the name in its technical sense: not a word of English grammar had

[33] For a full description of Mill's "elementary education," see his *Autobiography* (London: Oxford University Press, 1924), pp. 1–31.

been learned by me, not a lesson in composition. I had merely the ordinary knowledge of arithmetic; and, beyond that, no knowledge of mathematics. Of English history nothing; of ancient history a little; of ancient literature in translation nothing; of biography nothing.

This conspicuous absence of what were at the time regarded as important ingredients of a general education was, however, counterbalanced by what Spencer's father and Spencer himself considered a most valuable basic intellectual training.

Concerning things around, however, and their properties, I knew a good deal more than is known by most boys. My conceptions of physical principles and processes had considerable clearness; and I had a fair acquaintance with sundry special phenomena in physics and chemistry. I had also acquired, both by personal observation and by reading, some knowledge of animal life, and especially of insect life; but no knowledge of botany, either popular or systematic. By miscellaneous reading a little mechanical, medical, anatomical, and physiological information had been gained; as also a good deal of information about the various parts of the world and their inhabitants.[34]

In spite of obvious differences in the subject-matter studied, both Spencer and Mill felt that one of the greatest benefits they derived from their early education was rigorous "mental discipline." In part they attributed this to the method of their fathers. Thus Mill felt strongly indebted to his father for his insistence on the dissecting of arguments to see the reasoning behind them and on the utility of syllogistic logic itself in the individual's mental cultivation.[35] The method used by Spencer's

[34] *Autobiography*, I, 100.
[35] Mill, *op. cit.*, pp. 15–17, 25–26. Needless to say, Mill disagreed with Spencer about the importance of Latin and Greek in any scheme of general education.

father was primarily one of "prompting to intellectual self-help." Always asking for the natural cause of something, the elder Spencer sought to foster in his son "that same independence of judgment which he had himself."[36] Spencer felt that the discipline provided by mathematics, in which he always had an interest, strengthened his "reasoning powers."[37] In recalling the approach of his father, Spencer was in reality reflecting his own views, developed more fully in his educational essays, concerning what the proper educational method should entail:

If he did not make mental development a subject of deliberate study, yet he had reached some general ideas concerning it, and saw the need for adjusting the course of instruction to the successive stages through which the mind passes. . . . Always he aimed to insure an intelligent understanding of that which he taught: never being content with mere passive acceptance of it. And perceiving how involved a process is the unfolding of intellect, how important it is that the process should be aided and not thwarted, and what need there is for invention and judgment in the choice of means, he saw that, carried on as it should be, the educator's function is one which calls for intellectual powers of the highest order, and perpetually takes these to the full.[38]

Spencer had, for all practical purposes, completed his "formal education" by the age of thirteen. At that age he was placed under the educational tutelage of Thomas Spencer, his uncle, who tutored pupils in preparation for higher education. In his uncle's "school" he was exposed to Latin and Greek, in which his progress was "extremely small," and to Euclid and trigonometry, which he liked. In recollecting the status of his education at the age of sixteen, Spencer expressed almost the same impressions

36 *Autobiography*, I, 101.
37 *Ibid.*, p. 13.
38 *Ibid.*, p. 137.

as when he was thirteen. Except for mathematics and his natural inclination toward "mechanical" pursuits, he was quite deficient in literature, history, English grammar, and knowledge of the "concrete sciences."[39] At the age of seventeen Spencer deliberated about whether he should become a teacher like his father, but decided to become an engineer instead. He felt that his dislike for "mechanical routine," the unavoidable monotony that is involved in teaching, and his propensity toward pursuing his own unorthodox ideas about education would render him an unsuccessful teacher, disagreeable to his students' parents.[40] While engaged as an engineer (1837 to 1841), his interest in mathematics and scientific questions overweighed those in other areas.[41] After an interruption of about four years (1841 to 1845), he returned to his engineering profession for another three years. But it was clear that Spencer had become engrossed in other pursuits and now considered engineering primarily a means of earning a living. Finally he abandoned the profession altogether and threw himself "with a fearless courage and a radical thoroughness" into the social, political and religious discussions of the day. He had, in his own words, embarked upon a career in "literature," by entering the "press gang" class;[42] however, his abiding interest

[39] *Ibid.*, pp. 113–133, 149.

[40] *Ibid.*, pp. 140–141.

[41] His biographer writes: " 'I do not know what my mother will say to such a mathematical letter as this,' was a remark he might have made regarding more letters than one" (*Life and Letters*, I, 30). It was also during this "nomadic period" of his life that he read Lyell's *Principles of Geology*, which introduced "a fact of considerable significance in his life." Ironically, Lyell's refutation of Lamarck's hypothesis "that the human race has been developed from some lower race" had created in Spencer a greater leaning toward the Lamarckian position.

[42] *Ibid.*, pp. 44–48.

in scientific questions was maintained and increasingly strengthened. The range of his intellectual activities is well-illustrated by the diverse areas in which he wrote: science, economics, philosophy, psychology, ethics, sociology, education, music, and manners. Following his childhood education described previously, much of Spencer's education or "culture," as he often called it, was of the nature of self-education. His reading, which more often than not was cursory rather than systematic, covered a wide area ranging from phrenology to Carlyle's *Sartor Resartus*, Kant's *Critique of Pure Reason*, Coleridge's *Idea of Life*, Thomas Wyse's *Education Reform*, and James Pillan's *Principles of Elementary Teaching*. Many people wondered how Spencer was able to write on subjects about which he had read so little.[43] Spencer's biases in the materials he read and his reading habits remained the same throughout his life. A frequent visitor to the Athenaeum Club, he described a day's visit there as follows:

Having already glanced through *The Times* after breakfast, the news-room did not detain me. . . . Commonly some little time was spent in the drawing room in glancing through the contents of the Monthly Magazines and Quarterly Reviews: skipping most articles and dipping into a few. I rarely read one through. . . . Biographies, Histories, and the like, I commonly passed over without opening them. Books of travel had an attraction for me; and I glanced through them with an eye to materials for my work. Passages telling me of the institutions, beliefs, characters, usages etc. of the uncivilized, I not unfrequently copied. Of course all the works treating on this or the other branch of Science, as well as those which dealt with philosophical questions, special or general, including those on Theology, were looked into. . . . Novels were temptations to be

43 James Collier wrote that Spencer "picked up most of his facts" through conversations, while leafing through periodicals in the Athenaeum Club, and from the "mass of sociological materials" supplied by his assistants (Royce, *op. cit.*, pp. 208–209).

resisted; for I dare not expend on them the needful amount of reading power. Once in a year, perhaps, I treated myself to one; and then I had to get through it in a dozen or more instalments.[44]

A SCIENTIFIC PEDAGOGICAL SPOKESMAN

During the period of "fearless courage and a radical thoroughness," when he considered himself a member of the "press gang" class, Spencer composed his most famous educational essays. By 1860, when he drew up the prospectus of his system of synthetic philosophy, his strictly pedagogical writings had been completed. In this connection it is interesting that the first book of Spencer's published in the United States, where subsequently he attained so much popularity, was a collection of his four famous pedagogical essays.[45] Spencer, however, considered his pre-synthetic philosophical writings, including those on education, as only a preparation for his magnum opus and indeed as part of his all-encompassing evolutionary view of man, society, and the universe. Therefore, we would be mistaking Spencer's purpose if we treated these essays without any consideration of his broader philosophy, as Lauwerys points out.[46] This

[44] *Autobiography*, II, 262–263.

[45] The well-known volume *Education: Intellectual, Moral, and Physical* was published by D. Appleton and Company in 1860 through the efforts of Edward Livingston Youmans, Spencer's "American friend." An English edition of the same essays was published in 1861 by G. Manwaring. Since then, these essays have been reprinted many times in both England and the United States. The most recent American edition of the complete essays appeared in paperback in 1963 (Paterson, N. J.: Littlefield, Adams and Co., 1963).

[46] See J. A. Lauwerys, "Herbert Spencer and the Scientific Movement," in A. V. Judges, ed., *Pioneers of English Education* (London: Faber and Faber Ltd., 1952), p. 177.

would be even more true of Spencer's other statements
on educational problems, particularly on "political education," "national education," and the "bureaucratiza-
tion of education."

Such sets of problems lead us to another dimension of
Spencer's educational thought which has not received as
much attention as the pedagogical dimension. Almost
invariably comments on Spencer's educational ideas have
been restricted to his statements about the curriculum,
especially his advocacy of scientific education, the method
of education, moral education, and physical training,
that is, to the four essays mentioned previously. Occasionally some references are made to the political and
sociological dimensions of Spencer's educational thought,
but even these are limited to such stereotyped labels as
"private education," "utilitarian education," etc. In spite
of certain qualifications, it will be the contention later in
this essay that it is precisely in these political and sociological aspects of Spencer's educational views, which have
long been regarded as obsolescent, that Spencer's theorizing is most challenging for us today.

As a pedagogical publicist or reformer Spencer has
usually been associated with what has been called the
"scientific movement in education" because of the high
place he accorded to "science" in the content and method
of instruction. Spencer's views on this subject are force-
fully expressed in the selections included in this volume.
We will comment here upon his rationale and the educational context in which his views were expressed,
which centers in a controversy about the relative value of
scientific and classical studies, not far removed from the
"two-culture" theme discussed today.

Spencer's most pertinent and widely-referred to essay
is "What Knowledge Is of Most Worth?" published in the

Westminster Review in 1859. In an aggressive and vigorous tone, Spencer argues that the most valuable type of "culture" for the attainment of "complete" and "happy living"—the essential purpose of education—is "scientific culture," which he interprets as training in the physical and biological sciences, as well as in what we might today call the social sciences. Spencer reasons as follows: (a) Human life is constituted in terms of certain "kinds of activity," which he classifies in a hierarchical order of importance; (b) the aim of an ideal education should be preparation for all these activities; (c) since "in our phase of civilization" it is not possible to provide a "complete preparation" in all types of knowledge for all types of activities, the educational aim should be "to maintain *a due proportion* in the degrees of preparation in each"; (d) the value of knowledge to be included in a "rational curriculum" of the schools should be judged by the extent to which it can be shown to have "a bearing upon some part of life," that is, upon the activities which constitute life; and (e) scientific knowledge and culture, in the general meaning of the term, being of greater relative value or worth, should be assigned a preeminent place in the school curriculum. In addition to this "utilitarian" type of argument, Spencer justifies science on "disciplinary," moral, and even religious grounds. "Thus," he concludes, "to the question we set out with—What knowledge is of most worth?—the uniform reply is—Science. This is the verdict on all the counts."[47]

Weaknesses and limitations in Spencer's reasoning have been pointed out repeatedly by several writers. One early assessment of Spencer's views by R. H. Quick is particularly noteworthy, first, because of its perceptive-

[47] *Essays, Etc.*, p. 42.

ness, and second, because it sets the tone for many subsequent evaluations. This analysis was widely read by teachers and educationalists in the United States and in England. In the revised edition of his *Essays on Educational Reformers*, first published in 1868, Quick justifiably took pride in being one of the first people who recognized the value of Spencer's educational essays.[48] But he also found several inadequacies in Spencer's thought. Referring to Spencer's argument that for purposes of developing intellectual faculties no distinction is warranted between "useful knowledge" and knowledge needed as "a mental gymnastic"[49] and that scientific culture provides all that is necessary for mental discipline at all stages of education, Quick raised the objection that at different stages in the development of the child "different subjects must be used to train the faculties." He denied that there is *one kind of knowledge,* scientific or otherwise, which "is universally and at every stage in education, the best adapted to develop the intellectual faculties."[50] Turning to preparation for "complete living," and to Spencer's view that certain sciences can best prepare for the several activities or functions an individual will perform in society, viz., as parent, citizen, worker, etc., Quick rebutted that some such sciences would be beyond the children's understanding. Further, according to Quick, it is not clear that what Spencer considers "useful" knowledge, and by implication what he regards

[48] Robert Herbert Quick, *Essays on Educational Reformers* (New York: D. Appleton and Co., 1890), p. 439. So far as this writer has established, Quick was the first who saw fit to include Spencer among eminent educational reformers.

[49] At the time Spencer was writing a prevalent view was that the directly useful subjects were not necessarily the best for purposes of mental discipline.

[50] Archer, *op. cit.,* pp. 121–122.

"useless" and "ornamental," is necessarily the case. To know about the "Eustachian tubes," although helpful in understanding the normal rate of pulsation—a physiological fact—does not necessarily "influence action," or help one to "self-preservation," any more than knowing the proper pronunciation of Iphigenia. Even if one accepted Spencer's assumption that mathematics, physics, and biology underlie "all the practical arts and business of life," one would still have to grapple with the problem of what influence this consideration should have upon education. Quick asked: Should all these sciences be taught to everybody? Should there be different schools for different callings? Or should schools aim at sending children into the world with "a love of knowledge," and "a mind well disciplined to acquire knowledge," rather than with "any special information?"[51]

In his vitriolic criticisms of contemporary education, Spencer paid particular attention to what may be called "education for citizenship." In this connection he vehemently attacked the type of history commonly taught in the schools. Rather than being focused on "the right principles of political action" or "the science of society," history teaching was limited to narratives of conquests, to "court intrigues, plots, usurpations or the like, and with all the personalities accompanying them." Of what aid or value, Spencer asked, are such "facts" in "elucidating the causes of national progress," or in one's future "conduct as a citizen?" Further, that people are interested in such historical facts is "no proof of their worth."[52] This type of history, therefore, Spencer would relegate to the "leisure-part" of education, that is, the least important. Instead he called for the study of "the natural history of

51 *Ibid.*, pp. 442–445.
52 *Essays, Etc.*, pp. 26–27.

society" and of the structure and function of social institutions, in short, for the study of "descriptive sociology" and "comparative sociology."[53]

Quick objected to such categorical statements and assumptions concerning "education for citizenship." For
one thing, according to him, "we are completely at sea"
about the "right principles of political action," and for
another, Spencer ignored the *indirect* value of the type
of history he rejected. The value of narrative history,
Quick maintained, may be likened to that of travelling:
It "widens the student's mental vision, frees him to some
extent from the bondage of the present, and prevents his
mistaking conventionalities for laws of nature." Quick's
comments about Spencer's theory of history teaching are
trenchant and pedagogically sound, in this writer's opinion:

It is difficult to estimate the value of history according to Mr.
Spencer's idea, as it has yet to be written; but I venture to
predict that if boys, instead of reading about the history of
nations in connection with leading men, are required to study
only "the progress of society," the subject will at once lose all
its interest for them; and, perhaps, many of the facts communicated will prove, after all, no less unorganisable than the
fifteen decisive battles.[54]

Spencer's and Quick's views highlighted some of the
main points of an educational controversy which, although dating further back, reached a high pitch in the
decade following Darwin's *The Origin of Species* and
Spencer's provocative essay "What Knowledge Is of Most
Worth?" In the words of John Stuart Mill, "The great
controversy of the present day is the vexed question between the ancient languages and the modern sciences and

[53] *Ibid.*, pp. 27–29.
[54] Quick, *op. cit.*, pp. 448–450.

arts; whether general education should be classical—let me use a wider expression, and say literary—or scientific."[55] In this debate both extreme and middle-of-the-road viewpoints were expressed by a great number of the most notable intellectuals of the period. These included, in addition to Spencer and Mill, eminent scientists like T. H. Huxley, J. Tyndall, C. Lyell, J. Hooker and R. Owen; classical scholars like F. W. Farrar, H. Sidgwick, and Robert Lowe, who was also the *enfant terrible* of the Liberal Party; popular essayists and poets like Matthew Arnold and John Ruskin; and a host of headmasters and masters of eminent public schools (for example, Dr. Moberly of Winchester, the Reverend E. Balston of Eton, and J. M. Wilson of Rugby and later of Clifton).[56]

In his views on scientific studies or culture Spencer championed, in a rather extreme form, a cause which had several other noted adherents. T. H. Huxley, to take but one example, in the 1850's deplored the general status of science and science teaching in England. Even among the most highly educated persons, Huxley said in 1854, there is "utter ignorance as to the simplest laws of their animal life."[57] In the same year, Huxley defended the natural history sciences on "disciplinary," "utilitarian," aesthetic, and moral grounds. "I cannot but think," Huxley stated, "that he who finds a certain proportion of pain and evil inseparably woven up in the life of the

55 J. S. Mill, *Inaugural Address Delivered to the University of St. Andrews, February 1, 1867* (Boston: Littell and Gay, 1867), p. 5.

56 For a full discussion of this controversy, see Andreas M. Kazamias "What Knowledge Is of Most Worth? An Historical Conception and a Modern Sequel," *Harvard Educational Review*, XXX (Fall, 1960), 307–330. Some parts of what follows here were taken from this article.

57 T. H. Huxley, "On the Educational Value of the Natural History Sciences," *Collected Essays* (New York: D. Appleton and Co., 1894), III, 89–90.

very worms, will bear his own share with more courage and submission."[58] Likewise, Huxley called for greater emphasis upon the "theory of political and social life," and a type of history which would not be "a mere chronicle of reigns and battles, but as a chapter in the development of the race, and the history of civilization."[59]

Such views, however, should not be construed as implying that there were no differences between Huxley and other scientists, and Spencer. Huxley, in particular, was much more flexible in his thinking about the content of education. Like Spencer, he wished to see a radical change in the content and method of the curriculum of the schools, the most important being the introduction of scientific studies and a scientific way of examining knowledge.[60] Yet Huxley constantly urged that there should be a balance between scientific and literary-humanistic training. "The value of the cargo," he cautioned, "does not compensate for the ship's being out of trim."[61] Bibby sums up Huxley's views as follows: "In advocating a complete *bouleversement* of the existing

[58] *Ibid.*, pp. 92–93. Other evidence of Huxley's views on the value of science—even its religious value—is legion. Specifically, see his *Science and Education: Essays* (New York: D. Appleton and Co., 1894), pp. 114–125, 183–187, and his *Lay Sermons, Addresses and Reviews* (New York: D. Appleton and Co., 1871), pp. 88–89. On one occasion Huxley said: *"Sartor Resartus* led me to know that a deep sense of religion was compatible with the entire absence of theology. Secondly, science and her methods gave me a resting place independent of authority and tradition. Thirdly, love opened up to me a view of human nature, and impressed me with a deep sense of responsibility." (See C. Ayres, *Huxley* [New York: W. W. Norton and Co., 1932], p. 111.)

[59] Huxley, *Science and Education: Essays,* p. 184.

[60] "The modern world is full of artillery," Huxley said on one occasion, "and we turn out our children to do battle in it equipped with the shield and sword of an ancient gladiator" (*Lay Sermons, Addresses and Reviews,* p. 118).

[61] Huxley, *Science and Education: Essays,* pp. 153–154.

system, he looked upon English literature and history and political economy as having the same claims as natural science, and these four subjects he would make the common foundation of all education."[62]

In the melee of arguments that characterized the "great controversy" of the mid-Victorian era, at least two are worthy of further comment: knowledge for mental discipline and the usefulness of education. The concept of mental discipline, or the "mental-gymnastics argument," constituted the most important explicit element of the rationale which justified the inclusion of a subject in a program of liberal education. Traditionally it was assumed that the study of the classics had the unique attribute of training certain "faculties" of the mind, such as memory and reason, a doctrine which was based in part on what came to be known as "faculty psychology." In the controversy of the 1850's and the 1860's it is interesting to notice that few people, if any, disputed the concept that for a subject to be of any educational value it must have "disciplinary" value. Consequently, proponents of scientific education, such as Spencer, Huxley, Faraday, and Tyndall, sought to prove that science afforded mental training or discipline as well as the classics. In other words they sought to justify the claims of science on a rationale often associated with the classics. But one should guard against the imputation that all the educational writers of this time, especially the aforementioned ones, subscribed to this rather metaphysical concept of mind or to the faculty psychology which later became the target of philosophers and psychologists. Spencer, in particular, often talked about mental discipline, mental faculties, and training of judgment, memory, observation, etc, but for him these commonly used

[62] Bibby, *op. cit.*, p. 41. Also see pp. 255–256.

educational concepts did not imply a psychological theory by which the mind was envisaged in terms of compartmentalized units that could be formally trained like the muscles of the body. Indeed, such a psychological theory would have been quite contrary to Spencer's evolutionary concept of mind and intelligence. The development of mind and intelligence, the psychical part of life, according to Spencer, corresponded to the development of "external coexistences and sequences"; indeed it was related to such an external environment as cause and consequence.[63] It followed that mental faculties, such as ability to abstract, to generalize, to see relations, to "rationalize," to discriminate, to imagine, etc., could not develop or evolve "in the absence of a fit environment." The difference between "developed" and "undeveloped" or primitive people or societies, according to Spencer, is a difference in the degree of "social advance" and *a fortiori* of intellectual or mental advance. The mind or faculties of children, Spencer argued, are analogous to the minds or faculties of the uncivilized primitive savages: unable to abstract, to imagine constructively, to deal with complex relations, etc.[64] In order to train or develop children's faculties in a socially advanced environment one must follow the order of evolution. Education is possible, Spencer elaborates further in his essay "Intellectual Education," when matter and method "correspond with the order of evolution and mode of activity of the faculties." The basic pedagogical principles, which must be grounded on the basic evolutionary principles,

[63] See Spencer, *The Principles of Psychology* (New York: D. Appleton and Co., 1880), I, 407 ff.

[64] Spencer's views concerning the mental state of primitive people and how it corresponds with that of children are found in his *The Principles of Sociology* (3rd ed.; New York: D. Appleton and Co., 1892), I, pp. 73 ff.

are that education must proceed from the simple to the complex, from the indefinite to the definite, and from the empirical to the rational; further, it must "accord both in mode and arrangement with the education of mankind, considered historically"; it should encourage "self-development"; it must be pleasurable; and it must evoke the interest of the learner. It is clear that Spencer rejected the educational doctrine, often associated with faculty psychology, that the *form* of a particular area of knowledge, as well as the difficulty of the subject, trained specific faculties, irrespective of content. On another occasion he wrote: "Everywhere throughout creation we find faculties developed *through the performance of those functions which it is their office to perform;* not through the performance of artificial exercises devised to fit them for those functions."[65]

We now turn to the second frequently adduced argument, namely, that of "usefulness" in education. At the time Spencer was writing, the more directly useful a subject was regarded to be, the less its educational value was. It appears that, for purposes of a truly liberal education, the more a subject was perceived to contribute to mental and moral discipline or culture, the greater its educational "usefulness." To Spencer, it should be remembered, "usefulness" meant the degree to which an activity contributed to "complete living," which he regarded as the supreme aim of all education and which could be attained if education were directed toward five kinds of activity: direct self-preservation, indirect self-preservation, rearing and disciplining of offspring, maintenance of

[65] *Essays, Etc.,* p. 37. (Italics inserted by the editor.) In his *Autobiography* he wrote: "Throughout the organic world there goes on a process of adaptation by which faculties are fitted for their functions" (*Autobiography,* I, 241).

proper social and political relations, and "gratification of the tastes and feelings." Many have considered this viewpoint and the order of priorities given by Spencer sufficient reason to describe him as the advocate par excellence of utilitarianism. Indeed if the term utilitarianism is used to refer to the school of thought represented by such people as Bentham and Mill, then Spencer may be said to have been a supporter of the "principle of utility," or "happiness," as the ultimate criterion of all social action, including education, and this in spite of the fact that he criticized what he called the "expediency philosophy" of Bentham. When J. S. Mill, in his *Utilitarianism*, classified Spencer as an anti-utilitarian, the latter was "startled." He stated in a letter to Mill that his disagreement with the doctrine of utility was over "the method of reaching it" rather than "the object to be reached," viz., "happiness." He continued:

The Expediency-Philosophy having concluded that happiness is the thing to be achieved, assumes that morality has no other business than empirically to generalize the results of conduct, and to supply for the guidance of conduct nothing more than its empirical generalizations. But the view which I contend is, that Morality properly so-called—the science of right conduct—has for its object to determine *how* and *why* certain modes of conduct are detrimental, and certain other modes beneficial. These good and bad results cannot be accidental, but must be necessary consequences of the constitution of things; and I conceive it to be the business of moral science to deduce, from the laws of life and the conditions of existence, what kinds of action necessarily tend to produce happiness, and what kinds to produce unhappiness. Having done this, its deductions are to be recognized as laws of conduct; and are to be conformed to irrespective of a direct estimation of happiness or misery.[66]

[66] *Ibid.,* II, 100.

For Spencer, of course, the law of evolution provided the criterion of social action and morality, and the study of science (physical and biological) was necessary for the development of "the science of right conduct." As Aiken has pointed out, "it was not only the method of science which impressed him but the picture of the world and of man's place in it which was suggested by the substantive hypotheses of physical and, especially, biological science."[67]

"Utilitarian," however, has also been used to refer to Spencer's educational doctrine that a curriculum should be functionally related to the individual's future activities as a worker, a citizen, and a man of leisure. In this connection it is important to note that not even Spencer, let alone his contemporary scientific spokesmen, envisaged "usefulness" in education as "narrow utility," meaning direct preparation for a specific employment. More often than not, Spencer interpreted "usefulness" to mean that the content of education should take into consideration the individual as well as the social, political, and economic needs of an evolving industrialized, differentiated, and complex society. Moreover, it is imperative that Spencer's views be placed in their proper historical context. Many of the weaknesses that Spencer found deplorable in the education of his day have been eliminated; and some of the problems which were then significant do not possess the same cogency or relevance today. In short, our ideas about educational method, discipline, the upbringing of children, and curriculum content have changed. Under these circumstances, one could speculate that Spencer might have altered the order of priorities in his classification of the five "leading kinds of activity which constitute human life." When he

[67] Aiken, *op. cit.,* p. 163.

discussed "aesthetic" culture, for example, he explicitly stated: "So far from regarding the training and gratification of the tastes as unimportant we believe that in time to come they will occupy a much larger share of human life than now."[68]

Spencer, however, would not have retracted one essential principle, namely, that scientific culture should underlie all educational activities, be they of the nature of earning a livelihood or of enjoying leisure. To use C. P. Snow's terminology, he remained to the end a "one-culture" spokesman; the study of science was in accordance with his evolutionary view of life, his individualistic, nonconformist view of man, and his laissez-faire social theory.

SOCIAL EVOLUTIONIST AND INDIVIDUALISTIC EDUCATIONAL THINKER

Social evolution is particularly important in understanding Spencer's emphasis upon scientific culture and upon the principle of noninterference in the individual's education. His cumbersome definition of the law of evolution, included in the selections, may be paraphrased briefly in words frequently used in his writings: the tendency of all phenomena—organic, inorganic, and super-organic—to pass or "change" from the homogeneous and undifferentiated to the heterogeneous and differentiated. Influenced by Coleridge's "true idea of life" and Schelling's concept of a progressive development in organic

---

[68] *Essays, Etc.,* pp. 30–31. On this point see also Elsa Peverley Kimball, *Sociology and Education: An Analysis of the Theories of Spencer and Ward* (New York: Columbia University Press, 1932), pp. 145–146.

life toward differentiation and "individualization,"[69] Spencer formulated his own universal law of development and progress as follows:

Whether it be in the development of the Earth, in the development of Life upon its surface, in the development of Society, of Government, of Manufactures, of Commerce, of Language, Literature, Science, Art, this same evolution of the simple into the complex, through successive differentiations, holds throughout. From the earliest traceable cosmical changes down to the latest results of civilisation, we shall find that the transformation of the homogeneous into the heterogeneous, is that in which Progress essentially consists.[70]

Subsequently Spencer qualified this identification of change with progress by saying that evolution, and hence change for the better, was not inevitable. It was possible that "dissolution" rather than "evolution" would take place, depending on certain conditions. Implicit in this was the notion that evolution could be facilitated or inhibited. But the Victorians, Spencer included, apotheosized progress; hence it was inconceivable to them that the evolutionary metamorphosis could be checked and the process reversed.

A further element in Spencer's evolutionary hypothesis was integration, which follows differentiation. Certain likenesses in the functions performed by the differentiated units in a society, although creating tensions, ultimately tend toward some sort of integration or "equilibration," a characteristic of the most "advanced" societies. When development or evolution has progressed to this stage, a state of "social statics" has been reached, and the individual has attained perfect "equilibration" or "individuation." Under such circum-

stances, the individual automatically behaves as he ought
to behave, and hence there is no need for any compulsion or regulatory action. Spencer's social ideal, therefore, becomes one of complete anarchism, where the individual reigns supreme, and where freedom is ensured
by an inner moral commitment rather than by governmental regulation.

This theoretical model provided Spencer with what
he perceived as scientific validation of certain principles
of social and educational policy. In certain respects it
reinforced views which were "conditioned" in him by his
family background and his own educational experiences.
A traditional type of education, therefore, with its "unscientific" content and emphasis represented authority,
curtailment of the natural process of evolution, restric-
tion of individual freedom, and social control. In com-
menting further on his defense of scientific culture Spencer exclaimed:

Had Greece and Rome never existed, human life, and the right
conduct of it, would have been in their essentials exactly what
they now are: survival or death, health or disease, prosperity or
adversity, happiness or misery, would have been just in the
same ways determined by the adjustment or non-adjustment of
actions to requirements. And yet knowledge subserving the adjustment which so profoundly concerns men from hour to
hour, is contemptuously neglected.[71]

To Spencer scientific culture does not only "subserve"
the "adjustment" of man to his environment. It also frees
man from the shackles of tradition, authority, and dogmatism; it helps him to become a "discoverer," not a
"recipient," of knowledge; in short, it makes man realize
himself and his individuality. Literature, poetry, and the
arts, on the other hand, according to Spencer, represent

[71] *Autobiography*, II, 43.

the *social* rather than the *individual* aspects of life, and social interests often conflict with individual interests.[72] In so far as they also represent unquestioned truths about morality, they do not allow for independent judgment or "appeal to individual reason."

Spencer's emphasis on the unrestrained development of the individual, itself based on "the course of evolution," would seem to imply the total absence of any interference—from parents, teachers, government, etc. His argument might be reconstructed as follows: (a) Human beings and society as an "organism" evolve or develop, progressing *naturally* from the simple and undifferentiated to the complex and differentiated, and then to a state of integration; (b) in this natural process the individual is "integrated" or "equilibrated"—hence attaining a higher intellectual and moral state—by adaptation, that is, by modification according to the new functions required of him; (c) happiness, which is the ultimate end of this process and of life in general, can be attained if the individual expresses his right of liberty "to do all that his faculties naturally impel him to do"; (d) since freedom is a God-given right of all men, all men have "like claims" to exercise it, which may result in clashes of interests; (e) when such a situation arises, the individual's actions remain free to the extent that they do not interfere with the actions of others; that is, his freedom is restricted only by the equal freedom of others.[73]

In his cult of the individual Spencer assumed that as his faculties develop and as he leaves the predatory stage

[72] On this point, also see William Boyd, *The History of Western Education* (6th ed.; London: Adam and Charles Black, 1952), p. 371.

[73] See *Social Statics; or The Conditions Essential to Human Happiness Specified, And the First of Them Developed* (New York: D. Appleton and Co., 1873), p. 93. Also see *Autobiography*, I, 510–511.

of civilization, man acquires a sense of social justice and a sympathy for others. In addition, as man constantly adapts his nature to "the conditions of his existence," he progressively becomes more "moral" until his feelings "are in equilibrium with external forces they encounter." When such an equilibrium has been reached, "the individual has no desires but those which may be satisfied without exceeding his proper sphere of action, while society maintains no restraints but those which the individual voluntarily respects."[74] Such being the natural course of evolution, the function of social institutions, particularly of government or the State, must be to *protect* man's natural right of freedom by removing "political restrictions." In its ideal form, viz., the state of "social statics," there will be an "abolition of all limits" to the citizens' freedom.[75] "The ideally moral state," he later wrote, "was identified with complete adjustment of constitution to conditions; and the fundamental requirement, alike ethical and political, was represented as being the rigorous maintenance of the conditions to harmonious social co-operation; with the certainty that human nature will gradually be moulded to fit them."[76]

It is clear that Spencer interpreted freedom in a negative sense, namely freedom from restraint. This interpretation provided him with a theoretical justification for his pedagogical doctrines and his view about the proper role of government within education, namely the principle of noninterference. The idea that social control (compulsory or state education), although it

[74] *First Principles of a New System of Philosophy,* pp. 512–513.
[75] For a complete analysis of Spencer's political theorizing, see Sir Ernest Barker, *Political Thought in England 1848 to 1914* (Rev. ed.; London: Oxford University Press, 1947), pp. 70–112.
[76] *Autobiography,* II, 8.

might curtail the freedom of some, might also provide the conditions to enhance the freedom of others was relatively absent from Spencer's political ideology.

The more positive interpretation of freedom, which has provided a rationale for the modern welfare state and for more active government participation in social affairs, was already apparent in Spencer's lifetime. By the end of the nineteenth century, the utilitarian "philosophy of happiness" had ceased to occupy the respected position it held at the time of Bentham and, later, Mill and Spencer. Influenced by the German spirit of Kant and Hegel, British philosophical "idealists" like T. H. Green, Bernard Bosanquet, J. M. E. McTaggart, James Seth, and Edward Caird conceived of freedom, not in abstract negative terms, but in concrete positive terms, and of the state as a necessary agency for the improvement of man and the enhancement of his freedom. Bosanquet, for example, put it as follows:

> We must not treat the self as *ipso facto* annihilated by government; nor must we treat government as a pale reflection, pliable to all the vagaries of the actual self. Nor, again, must we divide the inseparable content of life, and endeavour to assign part to the assertion of the individual as belonging to self, and part to his impact on others, as belonging to government. . . . We must show . . . how man, the actual man of flesh and blood, demands to be governed; and how a government, which puts real force upon him, is essential, as he is aware, to his becoming what he has it in him to be.[77]

[77] Bernard Bosanquet, *The Philosophical Theory of the State* (London: Macmillan and Co., Ltd., 1910), pp. 77–78. For further criticism of the individualistic conception of freedom by Bosanquet, see *ibid.*, pp. 53–78. For a fuller exposition of the differences between the "individualists" and the "idealists," see Bertil Pfannenstill, *Bernard Bosanquet's Philosophy of the State: A Historical and Systematic Study* (Lund, Sweden: Hakan Ohlsson, 1936), pp. 90–116, 198–214. On the connection between English "idealism" and German "idealism" see *ibid.*, pp. 66–90 and Barker, *op. cit.*, pp. 16–69. For

Even among Spencer's mid-Victorian contemporaries, some of whom, in one way or another, were associated with the theory of evolution, there were important qualifications on the question of the role of the state in public policy, especially in educational policy. T. H. Huxley, for example, Darwin's own "bull dog," unlike Spencer, used the scientific doctrine of evolution to denounce the idea that the state was a worse bungler than any other "joint-stock company" (Spencer's words.) Huxley distinguished between natural and moral rights; and he maintained that, in order to guarantee the latter, which are characteristic of "rational man," the state must intervene, even compel, especially in the case of education. For, Huxley wrote, "it is a necessary condition of social existence that men should renounce some of their freedom of action; and the question of how much is one that can by no possibility be determined a priori."[78] In this connection one is reminded of the brush between Spencer and Huxley, who sacrificed their friendship in the interests of intellectual honesty. Huxley had consistently been critical of the "astynomocratic" (police) theory of the state and its extreme laissez-faire doctrines. But it was not until the late 1880's and the early 1890's that his views brought him into direct conflict with Spencer. In a series of letters and essays, and in his famous Romanes Lecture of 1893, Huxley directly and by implication in-

the views of T. H. Green, who was accounted to be the most influential teacher in Oxford since Newman, and who actively participated in educational, civic, and political affairs, see R. L. Nettleship, ed., *Works of T. H. Green* (London: Longmans, Green and Co., 1906), III, 371.

[78] T. H. Huxley, "Natural Rights and Political Rights," reprinted in M. Goodwin, ed., *Nineteenth Century Opinion* (Baltimore, Md.: Penguin Books, 1951), pp. 179–181. Also see his essays, "The Struggle for Existence," "On the Natural Inequality of Men," and "Government," in *ibid.*, pp. 204–206, 224, 230.

cluded Spencer in his attacks on "absolute ethics," "speculative arguments," and a priori political reasoning. Spencer was deeply hurt. This was especially true when Huxley said that the political philosophy based on the principle of noninterference entailed "the consistent application of which reasoned savagery to practice would have left the working classes to fight out the struggle of existence among themselves, and bid the State to content itself with keeping the ring."[79] "Reasoned savagery" Spencer felt to be "the unkindest cut of all." Using Huxley's words as the title, he wrote in a letter to the *Daily Telegraph*: ". . . for nearly fifty years I have contended that the pains attendant on the struggle for existence may fitly be qualified by the aid which private sympathy prompts. . . . Everyone will be able to judge whether this opinion is rightly characterised by the phrase 'Reasoned Savagery.' "[80]

Another close friend of Spencer's, the utilitarian John Stuart Mill, increasingly qualified his stand on state noninterference. In successive editions of his classic work *Principles of Political Economy*, he added more and more exceptions to the laissez-faire policy of government, one of which was a system of education.[81] Carlyle, Ruskin, and Matthew Arnold also found fault with strictly laissez-faire government.[82]

[79] For more details on Spencer's brush with Huxley, see *Life and Letters*, II, 27–37.

[80] *Ibid.*, p. 34. Duncan adds that Spencer's feelings were "bitter," especially since he had spent his lifetime "denouncing every form of oppression and injustice." And now to be accused of upholding "brutal individualism" and "reasoned savagery" was unthinkable.

[81] Mill, *Principles of Political Economy with Some of Their Applications to Social Philosophy* (London: Longmans, Green, and Co., 1920), pp. 953–956.

[82] See Thomas Carlyle, *Critical and Miscellaneous Essays* (New York: Charles Scribner's Sons, 1901), IV, 155; John Ruskin, *The*

Was Spencer naive enough to believe that Victorian England had reached the ideal state and therefore "no contrivance of statesmanship would achieve such beneficent results as might be trusted to emerge from a witch's brew of conflicting egotisms"?[83] Did his theory of a *natural* process of development or evolution completely exclude social planning, control, or guidance in order to facilitate the process? In education, in particular, is Spencer's system "decidedly too aristocratic," as Compayré characterized it?[84]

In attempting to shed some light on these questions, it is necessary to bear in mind that Spencer, unlike Darwin and Huxley, for example, was more of an ideological system-builder than a scientific inquirer or investigator.[85] Spencer, of course, constantly sought to ground his views in "scientific" evidence. But very often accuracy of facts or scientific objectivity was less important to him than the *relevance* or *significance* of such "facts," how "facts" fitted into general "laws," and to what extent they conformed to the absolute social ideal. The social and educational conditions of Victorian England did not conform to this ideal; they were a mere "transitional" stage in the evolutionary process.[86] But at the same time, the several

---

Works of John Ruskin, edited by E. T. Cook and A. Wedderburn (London: George Allen, 1904), X, 196; and Matthew Arnold, *The Works of Matthew Arnold* (London: Macmillan and Co., 1904), XII, 18, 38, 42–43, 53–57.

83 This phraseology was taken from Wingfield-Stratford, *op. cit.*, p. 59.

84 Gabriel Compayré, *The History of Pedagogy* (Boston: D. C. Heath and Co., 1895), p. 543.

85 This point made by Aiken is extremely important in understanding Spencer's social and educational views. See Aiken, *op. cit.*, p. 24.

86 See, for example, Spencer's introduction in Thomas Mackay, *A Plea for Liberty: An Argument Against Socialism and Socialistic Legislation* (New York: D. Appleton and Co., 1891), pp. 4–5, 24.

attempts to "improve" these conditions did not conform to the ideal either, for "improvement" assumed that what existed was not undesirable in all respects and that change meant *extending* rather than radically transforming what was already there. Being an ideological reformer, Spencer was not satisfied with changes in the mere "forms" of education; more importantly, attitudes and commitments to a way of life, or "character," must change too. Being a "scientific" thinker as well, he believed that such attitudinal changes could be effected through the content and method of the sciences. In short, in so far as Victorian education, or, more broadly, paideia, was concerned, it had to be turned "upside down." In propagating such views Spencer was making other assumptions which can be questioned, but our point here is that we would be misconstruing Spencer's intent if we described him merely as an enemy of "public" education, or conversely as an uncompromising devotee of "private" education and the evils associated with nineteenth-century laissez-faire liberalism. "Yes, education is the thing wanted," Spencer wrote in 1860, "but not the education for which most men agitate." Referring specifically to the type of education that would prepare men for "the right exercise of political power," Spencer raised a very important question which has by no means been satisfactorily answered.[87] The question may be phrased as follows: "What type of education provides the best preparation for participation in the polity or for the performance of one's functions as a citizen?" Spencer's answer, "Science," would probably be agreeable to many modern social science and social studies advocates. It seems to this writer that Spencer was justified

---

[87] Much of the current controversy concerning education for "political socialization" is particularly relevant here.

in criticizing the contemporary assumption that mere "Reading, Writing, and Arithmetic" fitted one for citizenship. Realizing that in time it was inevitable that the political influence of the populace would increase, he asked: "Should the masses gain a predominant power while their ideas of social arrangement and legislative action remain as crude as at present, there will certainly result disastrous meddlings with the relations of capital and labour, as well as a disastrous extension of State-administrations."[88] And in a revealing letter to J. S. Mill, dated March 25, 1859, shortly after Mill published his essay, *On Liberty*, Spencer's "slight dissent" on the question of education was expressed as follows:

Setting aside practical difficulties, which I expect would be considerable, I doubt whether education, of the elementary kind, is a trustworthy test of the intelligence requisite to give a vote. The mass of those who have the mere rudiments of education, are, I believe, as profoundly ignorant of all matters bearing on legislation as those who cannot read and write. By-and-bye, perhaps, as cheap newspapers spread, it may become otherwise; but at present I fancy this is the case.[89]

We might look at Spencer's social ideology from another viewpoint which is of considerable importance to the intellectual historian. It has often been held that Spencer's evolutionary thesis and his cult of individualism provided a theoretical justification for, coincided with, or reinforced a conservative social philosophy. This was particularly true, as Hofstadter says, of the reception of Spencer's ideas in the United States:

Conservatism and Spencer's philosophy walked hand in hand. The doctrine of selection and the biological apology for laissez faire, preached in Spencer's formal sociological writings and in a series of shorter essays, satisfied the desire of the select

[88] *Essays: Scientific, Political and Speculative* (New York: D. Appleton and Co., 1864), pp. 244–249.
[89] *Life and Letters*, I, 122.

for a scientific rationale. Spencer's plea for absolute freedom of individual enterprise was a large philosophical statement of the constitutional ban upon interference with liberty and property without due process of law. . . . The social views of Spencer's popularizers were likewise conservative. . . . Acceptance of the Spencerian philosophy brought with it a paralysis of the will to reform.[90]

Hofstadter has demonstrated, quite convincingly, the historical association between Spencerianism and American individualism and conservatism. But whether conservatism, the absence of a tendency toward social reform or of a "collectivistic" view of society, were or are the *inevitable* consequences of Spencerian ideology and the Spencerian approach is quite another matter. The influence of Spencerianism in the development of social thought is too vast a topic for our purposes here, but at least one illustration should suffice to suggest that Spencerianism was a complex of ideas, which, either in its totality or in some of its parts, had a variety of effects. We have already referred to the intimate relationship between Spencer and Beatrice Webb, the Fabian socialist. In the development of her thinking, Mrs. Webb felt indebted to Spencer for his insistence on probing into the "relevance" or "significance" of facts and for his emphasis on observing, classifying, and explaining social phenomena. Referring to Spencer's concept of "functional adaptation," she made the following pertinent observation:

This generalisation illuminated my mind; the importance of functional adaptation was, for instance, at the basis of a good deal of faith *in collective regulation* that I afterwards developed. Once engaged in the application of the scientific method to the facts of social organization, in my observations of East End life, of co-operation, of Factory Acts, of Trade

[90]Richard Hofstadter, *Social Darwinism in American Thought* (Rev. ed.; Boston: The Beacon Press, 1955), pp. 46–47.

Unionism, I shook myself completely free from *laissez faire* bias—in fact I suffered from a somewhat violent reaction from it.[91]

Spencer influencing a socialist! one may exclaim. Some of his contemporaries, for example Robert Buchanan and even Huxley, did not consider it inappropriate to apply the term "socialism" to Spencer's social ideal. Huxley's qualification was that Spencer was one of those socialists "only in the good and philosophical sense," which was not the case with communists.[92] Spencer, of course, objected to the description of his political views as "socialistic," for socialism to him had the makings of a tight bureaucratic system where everything would be completely regulated and regimented, allowing for no healthy competition of interests and for no individual freedom whatsoever. Unlike Marx and those who justified socialistic polities on the Marxist principle of evolution, Spencer considered socialism a development growing out of military dictatorships rather than liberal democracies and private enterprise. "My opposition to socialism" he remarked, "results from the belief that it would stop the progress to such a higher state and bring back a lower state."[93] A socialistic industrial society, according to Spencer, would create a type of bureaucratic aristocracy which would be no less restrictive and authoritarian than military despotisms, feudal states, or aristocracies of any kind. Such polities would brook no dissent or freedom of action but would be based on obedience and conformity.[94] A prophetic insight, one might add, considering what has happened in some socialistic states. It might also be viewed as a refreshing

91 Webb, *op. cit.,* p. 37.

92 *Life and Letters,* II, 32.

93 Mackay, *op. cit.,* p. 24.

94 On this point, also see Aiken, *op. cit.,* pp. 167–168.

plea for maintaining the freedom of the individual within large organized systems and bureaucratic controls, and this might include education as well. Yet perhaps it is not paradoxical that the apostle of science and individualism should have been found to be influential in shaping Beatrice Webb's thought. Establishing the laws of social organization and social behavior for the purpose of providing sound principles of social policy, which was germane to Spencerianism, might lead either to a conservative, laissez-faire, individualistic doctrine, or to a more positive evolutionary doctrine as in the case of the Fabians.

Finally, it is pertinent to point out that Spencer explicitly rejected the implication that the logical outcome of his pedagogical theory would be "complete laissez-faire." Drawing upon his usual "physical analogies," he argued that the more complex an organism, the longer the period of dependence on a "parent organism," as by analogy "every higher creature, and especially man, is at first dependent on adult aid." It followed, therefore, that it was the duty of adults to provide conditions "requisite to growth." Spencer concluded: "Hence the admission of the doctrines enunciated does not, as some might argue, involve the abandonment of teaching; but leaves ample room for an active and elaborate course of culture."[95]

PERSPECTIVES: HISTORICAL AND CONTEMPORARY

"No one reads Herbert Spencer nowadays," an English author wrote recently. Of the Victorians who in their time were celebrated at home and abroad, Spencer, per-

[95] *Essays, Etc.,* pp. 54–55.

haps the most renowned of all, "is almost alone . . . in being unread and having not even the ghost of a reputation." The same author scoffs at Spencer's "woolly generalizations" and "scientific" pretentiousness, and concludes that he is "justly forgotten."[96] It is true that today Spencer by no means enjoys the renown that he did during his time.[97] Certainly the description of Laevsky's romance in Chekhov's "The Duel," written in 1891, would today appear unromantic to say the least: "To begin with," says Laevsky, "we had kisses, and calm evenings, and Spencer, and ideals and interests in common."[98] In the field of education, where previously Spencer's views evoked bitter controversies, Spencer is hardly mentioned, except in some historical writings; and when mentioned, he is more often than not rejected.[99] Certainly in so far as American educational thought is concerned Spencer no longer is honored by men like William James, John Dewey, Josiah Royce, or Charles W. Eliot; nor by professional pedagogues, or national policy-making commissions.[100] But the fact remains that, from the appearance

[96] A. O. J. Cockshut, *The Unbelievers: English Agnostic Thought 1840-1890* (London: Collins Clear-Type Press, 1964), pp. 73-85.

[97] Hofstadter writes: "In the three decades after the Civil War it was impossible to be active in any field of intellectual work without mastering Spencer" *(op. cit., p. 33).*

[98] Quoted from J. Passmore, *A Hundred Years of Philosophy* (London: Gerald Duckworth and Co., Ltd., 1957), p. 39.

[99] An important exception to this statement is the excellent study by J. A. Lauwerys in Judges, *op. cit.,* pp. 160-194. The latest, most comprehensive study of Spencer's educational views was written in 1932 by Kimball. However this study is essentially expository, and its assessment of Spencer's impact is rather weak. An excellent edition of Spencer's famous educational essays, with a valuable introduction and critical notes, appeared the same year. See F. A. Cavenagh, ed., *Herbert Spencer on Education* (Cambridge, England: The University Press, 1932).

[100] For statements by James, Dewey, and Royce see: William James, *Memories and Studies* (New York: Longmans, Green and Co.,

of his essays on education in 1860 to the opening decades of the present century, Spencer was considered a great educational thinker and reformer, worthy of the utmost scrutiny and of inclusion in courses in pedagogy.[101] This is not the case today, an intriguing fact which raises the question, Why has Spencer suffered such a catastrophic fall?

A full explanation of this phenomenon would be an immense undertaking. Here we will simply offer some possible hypotheses which might provide the impetus for further dialogue and research.

It is not implausible to entertain certain hypotheses which, if fully substantiated, would be quite devastating to Spencer. One could maintain, for example, that Spencer's entire enterprise was a mistake from the beginning, so that after a quick flowering his reputation withered overnight when people came to their senses and realized that he had nothing to offer.[102] Hence one could infer

---

1912), pp. 107–142; John Dewey, *Characters and Events: Popular Essays in Social and Political Philosophy* (New York: Henry Holt and Co., 1929), I, 45–62; Josiah Royce, *op. cit.* Charles W. Eliot saw fit to write the introduction to the Everyman's Library edition of Spencer's *Essays on Education, Etc.* (1911). Concerning the controversies centering in some of Spencer's pedagogical ideas during the closing decades of the nineteenth century, see Jurgen Herbst, "Herbert Spencer and the Genteel Tradition in American Education," *Educational Theory*, XI (April, 1961), 99–111. Concerning "national policy-making commissions" or committees, the reference here is particularly to the Commission on the Reorganization of Secondary Education and its famous report, *Cardinal Principles of Secondary Education* (1918).

101 See Merle L. Borrowman, *The Liberal and Technical in Teacher Education: A Historical Survey of American Thought* (New York: Teachers College Press, Teachers College, Columbia University, 1956), pp. 41–72.

102 Cockshut has argued that Spencer's high reputation pointed to certain "very important and not very obvious weaknesses of the age in which it was enjoyed" (*op. cit.*, p. 85).

that any interest in Spencer would be "purely historical." This, of course, would be important in itself, but it would offer very little of universal significance to arouse interest or curiosity. Secondly, one could hypothesize that Spencer's educational reputation and popularity rested in large part on his reputation in other fields (philosophy, sociology, and psychology in particular); hence when these reputations collapsed, his educational reputation collapsed too.[103]

Although these hypotheses merit thorough investigation, certain considerations and observations indicate that it would be rather difficult to validate them. If one insisted that Spencer's ideas were worthless, how could one explain the facts that during the nineteenth century and the opening decades of the twentieth century Spencer was acclaimed by some of the most eminent intellectuals of the period;[104] that in his lifetime he was offered high honors, which he refused, by leading universities; that "he was continually applied to by men occupying public positions who were perplexed by social problems";[105] that he was "a personage in London society"; that during his visit to the United States he was triumphantly received by people from various walks of life (intellectuals, "managers

[103] In this connection R. L. Archer wrote: "But it was Spencer's reputation and not his arguments which produced the effect" (op. cit., p. 120).

[104] Reference has already been made to his reception in American circles. In England, to take but one of many examples, Huxley, in spite of his many disagreements, called Spencer "the most original of thinkers" (Webb, op. cit., p. 27). According to one source, Spencer elevated English philosophy in the nineteenth century to its previous heights. See Life and Letters, II, 281 ff.

[105] James Collier wrote: "Australians sought his counsel on the employment of black labor in the canefields, . . . New Zealanders desired his advice on the conflict between individualism and socialism" (Royce, op. cit., pp. 215–216).

of great railways," "hotel proprietors," etc.);[106] and that his books were translated into many foreign languages and sold in thousands.[107] Although Spencer's high reputation as an exponent of social evolution and as a philosopher heightened the interest in his views about education, it is important to remember that his first book published in the United States was *Education: Intellectual, Moral, and Physical*. At that time Spencer was known to some American audiences through his other essays and his *Social Statics* (1850), published in England. But his views on "scientific culture" and pedagogy were considered to be particularly significant for the American proponents of science and for improved methods of teaching.[108] Spencer, as noted earlier, was included among

---

[106] *Ibid.*, p. 227.

[107] D. Appleton and Company, his American publisher, noted that from 1860, when Spencer was first published in the United States, to 1903, 368,755 volumes of his works were sold, "not counting the sale of unauthorized editions during the years previous to the adoption of International copyright" (*Autobiography*, II, 113). Spencer's educational essays were translated even into Greek, an ironic twist considering Spencer's views on the study of Greek.

[108] As an illustration of this, the views of E. L. Youmans, Spencer's friend and a noted popularizer of science in America, are pertinent. Youmans' first acquaintance with Spencer's writings was in 1856 when he chanced upon *The Principles of Psychology*. Having been greatly impressed, he then read *Social Statics* and the various essays. In 1860 he sent his first letter to Spencer offering his help to have Spencer's books (those written and those proposed) published in the United States. But Youmans' immediate request was for permission to include two of Spencer's essays on education ("Intellectual Education," and "What Knowledge Is of Most Worth?") in a proposed volume of addresses by eminent scientists, "designed to present the increasing claims of science upon teachers and the directors of education" (John Fiske, *Edward Livingston Youmans: Interpreter of Science for the People* [New York: D. Appleton and Company, 1894], pp. 104–108). This volume appeared in 1867, but with another of Spencer's contributions. See E. L. Youmans, ed., *The Culture Demanded by Modern Life* (New York: D. Appleton and Co., 1867). In the meantime, however, Youmans was responsible

famous educational reformers by R. H. Quick as early as
1868. Quick's treatment centered exclusively in Spencer's
pedagogical significance, not his significance as a proponent of the law of evolution, or as a sociologist or a philosopher. It would be appropriate also to mention that
Spencer's educational essays were perhaps the most widely
read of all his publications. Certainly their success was
immense.[109] Even after Spencer's eclipse, the book that
reappeared most often in different editions was the one
on education.[110]

In seeking to provide possible explanations of Spencer's "downfall," one might follow a different line of
hypothesizing. One could advance the view that in the
field of education Spencer was merely echoing what was
already "in the air," dealing with burning issues of his
time, and that his appeal stemmed from the aggressive,
radical tenor of his writing rather than from any substantive additions he made to what was being said. Hence,
when certain educational issues lost their salience, so
did interest in Spencer.

---

for having Spencer's four essays on education published as a separate volume in 1860. In another letter to Spencer dated October
5, 1860, Youmans considered the educational essays as the most
suitable "introduction of its author to our people," for he felt that
they included a "masterly exposition of the educational claims of
science." Youmans continued: "We do not exactly know about that
'Unknowable'; we have great faith in it undoubtedly, but we are
sure of the weapon in hand and would prefer to open the cam-
paign with it" (Fiske, *op. cit.*, pp. 112–113).

109 Lauwerys notes: "Between 1878 and 1900, 42,000 copies of the
cheap edition (at 2s. 6d.) had been sold. In addition, 7,000 of the
ordinary edition at 6s. This apart from the American editions."
(Lauwerys, *op. cit.*, p. 161.)

110 In the United States the most recent edition was in paperback
in 1963: *Education: Intellectual, Moral, and Physical* (Paterson,
N. J.: Littlefield, Adams and Co., 1963).

Take, for example, Spencer's vigorous pleas on behalf of "scientific culture"—as an appropriate ingredient for the curriculum of the schools, as a useful type of education, and as a "disciplined" mode of inquiry. In the United States all these aspects of science were being debated in varying degrees before and after Spencer "joined the chorus." When, in 1867, E. L. Youmans edited a series of essays and addresses by noted advocates of science, including Spencer, he maintained that one of the basic questions confronting "the growing mind" of the United States was "what kind of culture" it should have. He went on to stress the fact that paying too little attention to "scientific subjects" was one of the "imperfections of the prevailing education in all its grades."[111] Likewise, in England, Huxley, as mentioned earlier, preceded Spencer in deploring the absence of scientific subjects in the education of the young, and Spencer's essay, "What Knowledge Is of Most Worth?" was purportedly a review of a collection of lectures emphasizing the claims of science given at the Royal Institution in 1854 and published the following year.[112]

This does not mean that Spencer made no original contributions to the discussion, but it does suggest that Spencer's ideas were part of a movement which already had its roots and which, at most, Spencer helped to popularize. In expanding and propagating the evolutionary doctrine, Spencer came to be regarded as the representative of what the *Atlantic Monthly* called the "scientific spirit of the age."[113] According to one writer, in the colleges and universities of America Darwinian and Spencerian ideas were rapidly accepted by scientific lead-

---

[111] Youmans, *op. cit.*, pp. v–vi.
[112] Lauwerys, *op. cit.*, p. 181.
[113] See Hofstadter, *op. cit.*, p. 33.

ers;[114] according to another, "Virtually every field of knowledge quickened under the influence of science in general and Darwinism in particular."[115] And, of course, Spencer had great influence on William Graham Sumner and Lester Ward.[116]

As time passed, however, the scientific spirit, of which Spencer was considered a major representative and of which he was an uncompromising spokesman, for all practical purposes gradually triumphed over the theological and even the humanistic one. In 1895 England's Royal Commission on Secondary Education, under the chairmanship of James Bryce, expressed fear that "a lopsided development" in favor of science was threatening to take place. About twenty years later, when the scientific-humanistic controversy erupted again, there were clear signs that classical education was entering a defensive stage. In his telegram to the participants in the Princeton Conference of 1917 on the place of classical studies in liberal education, Bryce was not merely reflecting his worries about what was happening in the United States; omens were equally inauspicious for classical education in England. Bryce's telegram read: "Rejoice to hear energetic efforts being made in America to vindicate place of classical studies."[117] Despite the slow

114 Theodore R. Sizer, *Secondary Schools at the Turn of the Century* (New Haven and London: Yale University Press, 1964), p. 33.

115 Lawrence A. Cremin, *The Transformation of the School: Progressivism in American Education, 1876–1957* (New York: Alfred A. Knopf, 1961), p. 91.

116 See Hofstadter, *op. cit.*, Chaps. III–IV.

117 Conference on Classical Studies in Liberal Education, *Value of the Classics* (Princeton: Princeton University Press, 1917). The controversy in England is more fully discussed in a forthcoming book by the present writer: *Politics, Society and Secondary Education in England* (University of Pennsylvania Press and Oxford University Press, 1966), Chap. XI.

progress of scientific subjects in entering the curriculum of the English schools, it would not be an exaggeration to assert that recently the humanities and the arts have been fighting a rear guard battle.[118] As in the United States, few people, if any, dispute the idea that science has a legitimate place in any scheme of liberal or general education. Therefore since the time of Spencer, the acuteness of the controversy over the place of science in education has been considerably blunted.

Yet the discussion of the "two-culture" theme continues today, and when modern American educators look back to the nineteenth-century spokesmen for science in the curriculum, they are likely to turn to people like Charles W. Eliot rather than to Spencer. Eliot, his biographer tells us, found much in Spencer to help him "clarify and formulate his ideas." Yet he "did not go all the way with Spencer and agree that science should be the universal staple of education in childhood."[119] Nor, we may add, did he accept the view that science should constitute the staple of education at any level. Likewise, Englishmen seem to be drawn more to Huxley and Arnold, among others, than to Spencer. It may be true that today educational writers prefer, as some Victorians did, "a reasonable, conciliatory, middle-of-the-way attitude" to Spencer's extreme, absolute, and intransigent one.[120]

---

[118] See Andreas M. Kazamias, "What Knowledge Is of Most Worth? An Historical Conception and a Modern Sequel," *loc. cit.*, pp. 324–330.

[119] Henry James, *Charles W. Eliot: President of Harvard University 1869–1909* (Boston and New York: Houghton Mifflin Co., 1930), I, 349–350.

[120] Lauwerys, *op. cit.*, pp. 188–189. Since Lauwerys delivered this lecture in 1951, the progress of science in the English schools has been much more rapid than he implies.

The preceding observations, however, lead to yet another line of reasoning: Spencer has been more or less forgotten in educational circles because, as Eliot,[121] Cremin,[122] and, in another context, Hofstadter[123] have implied, many of his ideas have been "thoroughly absorbed" in the evolving pedagogical language, theory, and practice. If this is the case, Spencer has become part of "conventional educational wisdom."[124] In tracing the development of ideas, under such circumstances, the original source and its influence are often lost sight of. Where controversy arises, references are made to individuals who espoused or articulated basically the same ideas as Spencer rather than to Spencer himself—or to individuals who modified Spencer, or indeed rejected him—but in each case he was an important source of the other's thought. In the United States, Spencer and the two famous NEA reports, the Report of the Committee of Ten, and the *Cardinal Principles of Secondary Education*, may be cited as examples of this "absorption" of the Spencerian views.

Spencer's influence, if any, on these important documents is still an open question.[125] In view of certain strik-

121 In his introduction to the 1911 edition, Eliot wrote: "Many schools, both public and private, have now adopted—in most cases unconsciously—many of Spencer's more detailed suggestions" (*Essays, Etc.*, p. xiii).

122 Cremin, *op. cit.*, pp. 90–94.

123 Hofstadter's reference is to Spencer's concept of individualism as part of the American national political tradition (*op. cit.*, p. 50).

124 Here I am indebted to Professor Merle Borrowman for the term and for the hypothesis. That there has been an "absorption" of Spencer's educational theories in our school systems seems also to be Kimball's view (Kimball, *op. cit.*, p. 125).

125 As yet we do not have convincing evidence about the precise nature of historical links between Spencer and these reports. Cremin, who points out this gap, assumes, quite logically, that Spencer was influential. He qualifies his statement by noting that on the ques-

ing similarities between Spencer's views and those expressed in these reports, the great reputation which Spencer enjoyed among the educational circles of the time, and the connections, direct or indirect, between him and key figures on the committees, it is only logical to assume a "filiation of ideas." This would be particularly true of the *Cardinal Principles of Secondary Education*. Barring any convincing evidence to the contrary, the great similarity between Spencer's "utilitarian" rationale as expressed in "What Knowledge Is of Most Worth?" and that of the report of the Commission on the Reorganization of Secondary Education would lead one to believe that by that time Spencer had so much entered the pedagogical vocabulary that his identity was lost; and continued to be lost thereafter.

There is, finally, a broader perspective against which Spencer's eclipse might be viewed. This is the change in the social and intellectual climate that began in the closing years of the last century and became predominant in the twentieth century. In the United States pragmatism and experimentalism provided a different rationale for social change, progress, education, and the advancement

tion of the disciplinary value of science, there was some divergence between Spencer's and Eliot's views. See Cremin, *op. cit.,* p. 93. This, however, is not absolutely correct. Spencer, in fact, viewed the sciences as being both "disciplinary subjects" and "directly functional." The difference between Spencer and Eliot on this point is more one of degree than of kind. See, for example, Spencer's *The Study of Sociology* (Ann Arbor: The University of Michigan Press, 1961) pp. 316–326, where Spencer speaks exclusively on the subject of science as "discipline." Also see Krug, *op. cit.,* p. 24. On Spencer and the *Cardinal Principles of Secondary Education,* Krug's conclusion is that if there was any "influence," it indirectly filtered through Kingsley, who, in turn, probably felt it through David Snedden, who had read lavishly in "Spencer, Huxley, and Darwin" (Krug, *The Shaping of the American High School* [New York: Harper and Row, 1964], pp. 400–402).

of knowledge from that of Spencer's evolutionary doctrine, although certain aspects of this doctrine were in-
corporated into the new philosophy. But, taken as a
whole, the new outlook raised questions for which
Spencerian answers could be of little practical value. In
the words of Hofstadter: "Pragmatism was absorbed into
the national culture when men were thinking of manipulation and control. Spencerianism had been the philosophy of inevitability; pragmatism became the philosophy
of possibility."[126] In the field of sociology, even evolutionary thinkers like Lester Ward drew different conclusions from Spencer's concerning social policy. Ward
placed more emphasis upon the "artificial" than the
"natural," and his cardinal social principle was "meliorism," that is, the purposeful improvement of social conditions through the application of scientific knowledge.[127] Empiricism, experimentalism, behaviorism, and
the idea of social control gradually impregnated and finally dominated social, educational, and political
thought, thus relegating Spencer to the position of a
publicist and visionary utopian.

As indicated earlier, a change of social and intellectual climate had also occurred in England. The temper
of the Edwardian era was very different from that of the
Victorian. In the sociopolitical realm, in Ensor's words,
"it was to be an age of democracy, of social justice, of

---

[126] Hofstadter, *op. cit.*, p. 123. Also see Gordon Lee, *Education
and Democratic Ideals: Philosophical Backgrounds of Modern Educational Thought* (New York: Harcourt, Brace and World, 1965),
pp. 109 ff.

[127] See Don Martindale, *The Nature and Types of Sociological
Theory* (Boston: Houghton Mifflin Co., 1960), p. 72. On the
educational dimensions of Ward's sociology, see Cremin, *op. cit.*, pp.
96–98. For a comparison between Spencer and Ward, see Kimball,
op. cit., pp. 284–314.

faith in the possibilities of the common man."[128]
In 1894, in a highly popular book, Benjamin Kidd, using
evolutionary concepts, argued that the interests of the
"social organism" or of "society" were greater and more
important than the interests of the individual, the latter
to be subordinated to the former.[129] In the philosophic
realm, the influence of German idealism was so great that
R. B. Haldane, a leading Liberal, could write: "The name
of the little territory which encloses Weimar and Jena
stirs the imagination of thousands of our youth of both
sexes, even as the name of Jerusalem moved the hearts
of men in the centuries behind us."[130] This was also the
period of socialist movements and the emergence of the
Labour Party in British politics. Robert Blatchford's
radical socialist journal *Clarion* enjoyed as much popularity as Cobbett's *Political Register* did earlier. In
Merrie England, a penny edition of a collection of essays
from the *Clarion,* which from 1894 to 1895 sold a million
copies, "practical socialism" was defined as "a kind of
scheme of co-operation, managed by the State." In obvious rebuttal to the philosophy of laissez-faire and unrestrained individualism (Spencer was actually mentioned in this connection), it was asserted that practical
socialism could do almost everything to improve the conditions of the people, from managing railways and
mines, to educating the people and providing food, amuse-
ment, even beer for them.[131] Further, by 1906, when the

128 R. C. K. Ensor, *England 1870–1914* (Oxford: At the Clarendon
Press, 1936), p. 527.

129 Benjamin Kidd, *Social Evolution* (London: Macmillan and
Co., 1895), pp. 84–85, 264. In four years this book ran into nineteen
editions.

130 R. B. Haldane, "Hegel," *Contemporary Review,* LXVII (February, 1895), 232 ff.

131 See J. F. C. Harrison, ed., *Society and Politics in England*

Liberal Party was returned to power, Liberalism as a
social philosophy had undergone a process of reconstruction. "Liberty," exclaimed H. H. Asquith, "is not only a
negative but a positive conception. Freedom cannot be
predicated, in its true meaning, either of a man or of
a society, merely because they are no longer under the
compulsion of restraints which have the sanction of positive law."[132] And L. T. Hobhouse, one of the leading
intellectual proponents of the "New Liberalism," wrote:

> . . . the struggle for liberty is also when pushed through a strug-
> gle for equality. Freedom to choose and follow an occupation,
> if it is to become fully effective, means equality with others in
> the opportunities for following such occupation.[133]

Samuel put it more bluntly: "It is the duty of the State
to secure to all its members, and all others whom it can
influence, the fullest possible opportunity to lead the
best life."[134]

As in the case of the United States, such a different
social and intellectual climate raised questions for which
Spencerian social philosophy did not seem to be practicable. And the trend toward social control, state inter-

---

1780–1960: A Selection of Readings and Comments (New York:
Harper and Row, 1965), pp. 311–315.

[132] See Herbert Samuel, *Liberalism: An Attempt to State the
Principles and Proposals of Contemporary Liberalism in England*
(London: Grant Richards, 1902), pp. ix–x.

[133] L. T. Hobhouse, *Liberalism* (New York: Henry Holt and
Co., 1911), p. 32. For a more detailed examination of this
theme, see Howard J. Thompson, "The New Liberalism in Great
Britain: The Liberal Mind and Party Politics in a Time of Crisis
and Reconstruction (1890–1914), Unpublished Ph.D. thesis, Harvard University, Cambridge, Mass., April 5, 1954.

[134] Samuel, *op. cit.*, p. 4. Samuel included "health, knowledge, and
material comfort" among the "positive aids" which would lead to
the "best life." And from this principle he deduced a policy of
social reform. (*Ibid.*, pp. 8–11.)

ference and a purposive social "meliorism" has accelerated throughout the subsequent decades. The welfare state philosophy continues to be a most powerful activating ideal in both countries. Under such circumstances, Spencerian social and political ideology, and the educational views which constituted an essential part of it, are numbered, as Eliza Cook had predicted of the *Social Statics,* among "the curiosities of literature."[135]

Yet, however true this may be, perspectives change. One need only say that Cockshut's verdict that Spencer is "justly forgotten" has the inherent weakness of assuming that historical judgments are final and absolute; and that we know what we need to know in order to make such judgments. Verdicts about Spencer, particularly in the field of education, would be considerably strengthened if our knowledge about his place in the development of ideas and practices was more complete. We have pointed to certain hypotheses that need to be explored further. It is possible that when this is done, Spencer's current reputation may improve. But even if on the basis of increased historical knowledge the present perspective remains, certain aspects of Spencer's social ideology, when separated from his teleological assumptions, may be found to be of considerable relevance for us today.

Modern polities and societies have become more structured, more planned, and more bureaucratized, a state of affairs often justified on the basis of equalitarian ideologies, distributive justice, social efficiency, and a more positive conception of human freedom. This *ideological* justification is as valid for democratic polities as for totalitarian-socialistic or communist ones. Modern liberal democracies, like England and the United States, al-

[135] See G. M. Young, *Victorian England: Portrait of an Age* (Garden City, N. Y.: Doubleday Anchor Books, 1954), p. 89.

though tending toward a planned social order, have sought to avoid complete regimentation and absolutism. To use Weberian language, they have sought to establish *rational* bureaucratic organizations where decision making is not in the hands of a self-perpetuating group and where individual freedom and opportunities are maintained. But, as has been pointed out several times, extension of bureaucratic control, however rational it may be, always presents the danger of regimentation and absolutism, and the creation of a calcified social system. Social efficiency, social control, and freedom need not necessarily complement each other; they may contradict or conflict with each other. It is in this connection that Spencer's passion for individualism and his clamor against undue bureaucratic control is significant for man in modern mass society. This does not necessarily mean an acceptance of Spencer's views as a guide to educational or social policy; but Spencer can generate in us what the distinguished French historian H. I. Marrou has called a sort of "dialogue" between "the Self and the Other." Such a dialogue, Marrou continues, "is simply a means of acquiring culture, enlarging our perspective and stripping us moderns of that naive self-sufficiency which prevents us from imagining that anyone could be different from ourselves."[136]

Further, in emphasizing so strongly the moral component of individual action rather than external conditions as a basis for the good society, Spencer confronts the educator and the educational policy-maker with a constant challenge. Harold Laski's comments on John Stuart Mill are applicable to Spencer as well. While

[136] H. I. Marrou, *A History of Education in Antiquity* (New York: Sheed and Ward, 1956; Reissued as a Mentor Book, 1964), pp. xii–xiii.

pointing to our modern emphasis on the "positive character of social control" for "the preservation of individuality," he insists that Mill's, and one might add Spencer's, ideal "is still as noble an ideal as a man may desire: the perception that the eminent worth of human personality is too precious to be degraded by institutions."[137]

[137] Mill, *op. cit.*, pp. xviii–xix.

1

*Individualism, Education,
and the Polity*

1. The Doctrine of Evolution*

"Here it was that on the 7th of May 1860, I began my undertaking; and here it was that I quickly furnished justification to any who exclaimed against my folly in attempting so great a task with my deranged health."†
The undertaking of which Spencer spoke was the writing of his synthetic philosophy, centered in the all-embracing concept of evolution—organic, inorganic, and superorganic—and attempting to unify all the sciences of the time. In view of the centrality of the doctrine of evolution in Spencer's ideology, a fitting introduction to it are some of his statements in the First Principles, *the first of his voluminous series on the subject.* First Principles *originally appeared in 1862 and was subsequently re-edited and revised at least six times. It contains the major "laws" and "propositions" of the theory of evolution, which he elaborated in the other volumes* (The Principles of Biology, The Principles of Psychology, The Principles of Sociology, *and* The Principles of Ethics). *In as much as it also deals with basic principles of the organization of society, this book has been ranked as one of the earliest treatises on sociology. Spencer's sociological treatment of institutions, particularly in terms of "structure" and "function," has earned him a place among the fathers*

---

* *First Principles of a New System of Philosophy* (2nd ed.; New York: D. Appleton and Co., 1868), pp. 18–19; 66–67; 396; 510–513; 545–549; 554–555. The subtitles were inserted by the editor.

† *Autobiography,* II, 69.

*of modern sociology. If separated from his teleological
assumptions and presuppositions, much of what he says
about social organization would sound very modern to
the "functionalist" comparative educators. It is also relevant to point out a recent trend among sociologists "to
reevaluate the evolutionary perspective in sociology."‡*

LAW OF EVOLUTION

Evolution is an integration of matter and concomitant
dissipation of motion; during which the matter passes
from an indefinite, incoherent homogeneity to a definite,
coherent heterogeneity; and during which the retained
motion undergoes a parallel transformation.

.   .   .

The law of Evolution has been thus far contemplated as
holding true of each order of existences, considered as a
separate order. But the induction as so presented, falls
short of that completeness which it gains when we contemplate these several orders of existences as forming
together one natural whole. While we think of Evolution
as divided into astronomic, geologic, biologic, psychologic,
sociologic, &c., it may seem to a certain extent a co-
incidence that the same law of metamorphosis holds
throughout all its divisions. But when we recognize these
divisions as mere conventional groupings, made to facilitate the arrangement and acquisition of knowledge—
when we regard the different existences with which they
severally deal as component parts of one Cosmos; we see
at once that there are not several kinds of Evolution

‡ See *American Sociological Review,* XXIX (June, 1964).

having certain traits in common, but one Evolution going on everywhere after the same manner. We have repeatedly observed that while any whole is evolving, there is always going on an evolution of the parts into which it divides itself; but we have not observed that this equally holds of the totality of things, as made up of parts within parts from the greatest down to the smallest. We know that while a physically-cohering aggregate like the human body is getting larger and taking on its general shape, each of its organs is doing the same; that while each organ is growing and becoming unlike others, there is going on a differentiation and integration of its component tissues and vessels; and that even the components of these components are severally increasing and passing into more definitely heterogeneous structures. But we have not duly remarked that, setting out with the human body as a minute part, and ascending from it to greater parts, this simultaneity of transformation is equally manifest—that while each individual is developing, the society of which he is an insignificant unit is developing too; that while the aggregate mass forming a society is becoming more definitely heterogeneous, so likewise is that total aggregate, the Earth, of which the society is an inappreciable portion; that while the Earth, which in bulk is not a millionth of the Solar System, progresses towards its concentrated and complex structure, the Solar System similarly progresses; and that even its transformations are but those of a scarcely appreciable portion of our Sidereal System, which has at the same time been going through parallel changes.

So understood, Evolution becomes not one in principle only, but one in fact. There are not many metamorphoses similarly carried on; but there is a single metamorphosis universally progressing, wherever the reverse metamorphosis has not set in. In any locality, great or small, throughout space, where the occupying matter acquires an appreciable individuality, or distinguishableness from other matter, there Evolution goes on; or rather, the acquirement of this appreciable individuality is the commencement of Evolution. And this holds uniformly; regardless of the size of the aggregate, regardless of its inclusion in other aggregates, and regardless of the wider evolutions within which its own is comprehended.

The first conclusion arrived at was, that any finite homogeneous aggregate must inevitably lose its homogeneity, through the unequal exposure of its parts to incident forces. It was pointed out that the production of diversities of structure by diverse forces, and forces acting under diverse conditions, has been illustrated in astronomic evolution; and that a like connection of cause and effect is seen in the large and small modifications undergone by our globe. The early changes of organic germs supplied further evidence that unlikenesses of structure follow unlikenesses of relations to surrounding agencies—evidence enforced by the tendency of the differently-placed members of each species to diverge into varieties. And we found that the contrasts, political and industrial, which arise between the parts of societies, serve to illustrate the same principle. The instability of the homogeneous thus everywhere exemplified, we also saw holds in each of the distinguishable parts into which any uniform whole lapses; and that so the less heterogeneous tends continually to become more heterogeneous.

A further step in the inquiry disclosed a secondary cause of increasing multiformity. Every differentiated part is not simply a seat of further differentiations, but also a parent of further differentiations; since, in growing unlike other parts, it becomes a centre of unlike reactions on incident forces, and by so adding to the diversity of forces at work, adds to the diversity of effects produced. This multiplication of effects proved to be similarly traceable throughout all Nature—in the actions and reactions that go on throughout the Solar System, in the never-ceasing geologic complications, in the involved symptoms produced in organisms by disturbing influences, in the many thoughts and feelings generated by single impressions, and in the ever-ramifying results of each new agency brought to bear on a society. To which was added the corollary, confirmed by abundant facts, that the multiplication of effects advances in a geometrical progression along with advancing heterogeneity.

Completely to interpret the structural changes constituting Evolution, there remained to assign a reason for that increasingly-distinct demarcation of parts, which accompanies the production of differences among parts. This reason we discovered to be, the segregation of mixed units under the action of forces capable of moving them. We saw that when unlike incident forces have made the parts of an aggregate unlike in the natures of their component units, there necessarily arises a tendency to separation of the dissimilar units from one another, and to a clustering of those units which are similar. This cause of the local integrations that accompany local differentiations, turned out to be likewise exemplified by all kinds of Evolution—by the formation of celestial bodies, by the moulding of the Earth's crust, by organic modifications, by the establishment of mental distinctions, by the genesis of social divisions.

At length, to the query whether these processes have any limit, there came the answer that they must end in equilibrium. That continual division and subdivision of

forces, which changes the uniform into the multiform
and the multiform into the more multiform, is a process
by which forces are perpetually dissipated; and dissipation of them, continuing as long as there remain any
forces unbalanced by opposing forces, must end in rest.
It was shown that when, as happens in aggregates of
various orders, many movements are going on together,
the earlier dispersion of the smaller and more resisted
movements, establishes moving equilibria of different
kinds: forming transitional stages on the way to complete equilibrium. And further inquiry made it apparent
that for the same reason, these moving equilibria have
a certain self-conserving powers; shown in the neutraliza-
tion of perturbations, and the adjustment to new conditions. This general principle of equilibration, like the
preceding general principles, was traced throughout all
forms of Evolution—astronomic, geologic, biologic, mental and social. And our concluding inference was, that
the penultimate stage of equilibration, in which the
extremest multiformity and most complex moving equilibrium are established, must be one implying the highest
conceivable state of humanity.

SOCIAL EQUILIBRIUM

One other kind of social equilibration has still to be
considered:—that which results in the establishment
of governmental institutions, and which becomes complete as these institutions fall into harmony with the
desires of the people. There is a demand and supply in
political affairs as in industrial affairs; and in the one
case as in the other, the antagonist forces produce a
rhythm which, at first extreme in its oscillations, slowly

settles down into a moving equilibrium of comparative regularity. Those aggressive impulses inherited from the pre-social state—those tendencies to seek self-satisfaction regardless of injury to other beings, which are essential to a predatory life, constitute an anti-social force, tending ever to cause conflict and eventual separation of citizens. Contrariwise, those desires whose ends can be achieved only by union, as well as those sentiments which find satisfaction through intercourse with fellow-men, and those resulting in what we call loyalty, are forces tending to keep the units of a society together. On the one hand, there is in each citizen, more or less of resistance against all restraints imposed on his actions by other citizens: a resistance which, tending continually to widen each individual's sphere of action, and reciprocally to limit the spheres of action of other individuals, constitutes a repulsive force mutually exercised by the members of a social aggregate. On the other hand, the general sympathy of man for man, and the more special sympathy of each variety of man for others of the same variety, together with sundry allied feelings which the social state gratifies, act as an attractive force, tending ever to keep united those who have a common ancestry. And since the resistances to be overcome in satisfying the totality of their desires when living separately, are greater than the resistances to be overcome in satisfying the totality of their desires when living together, there is a residuary force that prevents their separation. Like all other opposing forces, those exerted by citizens on each other, are ever producing alternating movements, which, at first extreme, undergo a gradual diminution on the way to ultimate equilibrium. In small, undeveloped societies, marked rhythms result from these conflicting tendencies. A tribe whose members have held together for a generation or two, reaches a size at which it will not hold together; and on the occurrence of some event causing unusual antagonism among its members, divides. Each primitive nation, depending largely for its continued union on the character of its chief, exhibits wide oscillations between an extreme in which the subjects are under rigid restraint, and an extreme in which the restraint is not enough to prevent disorder. In more advanced nations of like type, we always find violent actions and reactions of the same essential nature—"despotism tempered by assassination," characterizing a political state in which unbearable repression from time to time brings about a bursting of all bonds. In this familiar fact, that a period of tyranny is followed by a period of license and *vice-versa*, we see how these opposing forces are ever equilibrating each other; and we also see, in the tendency of such movements and counter-movements to become more moderate, how the equilibration progresses towards completeness. The conflict between Conservatism (which stands for the restraints of society over the individual) and Reform (which stands for the liberty of the individual against society), fall within slowly approximating limits; so that the temporary predominance of either, produces a less marked deviation from the medium state. This process, now so far advanced among ourselves that the oscillations are comparatively unobtrusive, must go on till the balance between the antagonist forces approaches indefinitely near perfection. For, as we have already seen, the adaptation of man's nature to the conditions of his existence, cannot cease until the internal forces which we know as feelings are in equilibrium with the external forces they encounter. And the establishment of this equilibrium, is the arrival at a state of human nature and social organization, such that the individual has no desires but those which may be satisfied without exceeding his proper sphere of action, while society maintains no restraints but those which the individual voluntarily respects. The progressive extension of the liberty of citizens, and the reciprocal removal of political restrictions, are the steps by which we advance towards this state. And the ultimate abolition of all limits to the freedom of each, save those imposed by the like freedom of all, must result from the complete equilibration between man's desires and the conduct necessitated by surrounding conditions.

Of course in this case, as in the preceding ones, there is thus involved a limit to the increase of heterogeneity. A few pages back, we reached the conclusion that each advance in mental evolution, is the establishment of some further internal action, corresponding to some further external action—some additional connection of ideas or feelings, answering to some before unknown or unantagonized connection of phenomena. We inferred that each such new function, involving some new modification of structure, implies an increase of heterogeneity; and that thus, increase of heterogeneity must go on, while there remain any outer relations affecting the organism which are unbalanced by inner relations. Whence we saw it to follow that increase of heterogeneity can come to an end only as equilibration is completed. Evidently the like must simultaneously take place with society. Each increment of heterogeneity in the individual, must directly or indirectly involve, as cause or consequence, some increment of heterogeneity in the arrangements of the aggregate of individuals. And the limit to social complexity can be arrived at, only with the establishment of the equilibrium, just described, between social and individual forces.

SCIENCE AND ITS LIMITATIONS

What is Science? To see the absurdity of the prejudice against it, we need only remark that Science is simply a higher development of common knowledge; and that if Science is repudiated, all knowledge must be repudiated along with it. The extremest bigot will not suspect any harm in the observation that the sun rises earlier and sets later in the summer than in the winter; but will rather consider such an observation as a useful aid in fulfilling the duties of life. Well, Astronomy is an organized body of similar observations, made with greater nicety, extended to a larger number of objects, and so analyzed as to disclose the real arrangements of the heavens, and to dispel our false conceptions of them. That iron will rust in water, that wood will burn, that long kept viands become putrid, the most timid sectarian will teach without alarm, as things useful to be known. But these are chemical truths: Chemistry is a systematized collection of such facts, ascertained with precision, and so classified and generalized as to enable us to say with certainty, concerning each simple or compound substance, what change will occur in it under given conditions. And thus it is with all the sciences. They severally germinate out of the experiences of daily life; insensibly as they grow they draw in remoter, more numerous, and more complex experiences; and among these, they ascertain laws of dependence like those which make up our knowledge of the most familiar objects. Nowhere is it possible to draw a line and say—here Science begins. And as it is the function of common observation to serve for the guidance of conduct; so, too, is the guidance of conduct the office of the most recondite and abstract inquiries of Science. Through the countless industrial processes and the various modes of locomotion which it has given to us, Physics regulates more completely our social life than does his acquaintance with the properties of surrounding bodies regulate the life of the savage. Anatomy and Physiology, through their effects on the practice of medicine and hygiene, modify our actions almost as much as does our acquaintance with the evils and benefits which common environing agencies may produce on our bodies. All Science is prevision; and all prevision ultimately aids us in greater or less degree to achieve the good and avoid the bad. As certainly as the perception of an object lying in our path warns us against stumbling over it; so certainly do those more compli-cated and subtle perceptions which constitute Science, warn us against stumbling over intervening obstacles in the pursuit of our distant ends. Thus being one in origin and function, the simplest forms of cognition and the most complex must be dealt with alike. We are bound in con-sistency to receive the widest knowledge which our fac-ulties can reach, or to reject along with it that narrow knowledge possessed by all. There is no logical alterna-tive between accepting our intelligence in its entirety, or repudiating even that lowest intelligence which we possess in common with brutes.

.   .   .

Ultimate Scientific Ideas, then, are all representative of realities that cannot be comprehended. After no matter how great a progress in the colligation of facts and the establishment of generalizations ever wider and wider— after the merging of limited and derivative truths in truths that are larger and deeper has been carried no matter how far; the fundamental truth remains as much beyond reach as ever. The explanation of that which is explicable, does but bring out into greater clearness the inexplicableness of that which remains behind. Alike in the external and the internal worlds, the man of science sees himself in the midst of perpetual changes of which he can discover neither the beginning nor the end. If, tracing back the evolution of things, he allows himself to entertain the hypothesis that the Universe once existed in a diffused form, he finds it utterly impossible to conceive how this came to be so; and equally, if he speculates on the future, he can assign no limit to the grand succession of phenomena ever unfolding themselves before him. In like manner if he looks inward, he perceives that both ends of the thread of consciousness are beyond his grasp; nay, even beyond his power to think of as having existed or as existing in time to come. When, again, he turns from the succession of phenomena, external or internal, to their intrinsic nature, he is just as much at fault. Supposing him in every case able to resolve the appearances, properties, and movements of things, into manifestations of Force in Space and Time; he still finds that Force, Space, and Time pass all understanding. Similarly, though the analysis of mental actions may finally bring him down to sensations, as the original materials out of which all thought is woven, yet he is little forwarder; for he can give no account either of sensations themselves or of that something which is conscious of sensations. Objective and subjective things he thus ascertains to be alike inscrutable in their substance and genesis. In all directions his investigations eventually bring him face to face with an insoluble enigma; and he ever more clearly perceives it to be an insoluble enigma. He learns at once the greatness and the littleness of the human intellect—its power in dealing with all that comes within the range of experience; its impotence in dealing with all that transcends experience. He realizes with a special vividness the utter incomprehensibleness of the simplest fact, considered in itself. He, more than any other, truly *knows* that in its ultimate essence nothing can be known.

.   .   .

If these conclusions be accepted—if it be agreed that the phenomena going on everywhere are parts of the general process of Evolution, save where they are parts of the reverse process of Dissolution, then we may infer that all phenomena receive their complete interpretation, only when recognized as parts of these processes. Whence it follows that the limit towards which Knowledge is advancing, must be reached when the formulae of these processes are so applied as to yield a total and specific interpretation of each phenomenon in its entirety, as well as of phenomena in general.

The partially-unified knowledge distinguished as Science, does not yet include such total interpretations. Either, as in the more complex sciences, the progress is almost exclusively inductive; or, as in the simpler sciences, the deductions are concerned with the component phenomena; and at present there is scarcely a consciousness that the ultimate task is the deductive interpretation of phenomena in their state of composition. The Abstract Sciences, dealing with the forms under which phenomena are presented, and the Abstract-Concrete Sciences, dealing with the factors by which phenomena are produced, are philosophically considered, the handmaids of the Concrete Sciences, which deal with the produced phenomena as existing in all their natural complexity. The laws of the forms and the laws of the factors having been ascertained, there then comes the business of ascertaining the laws of the products, as determined by the inter-action of the co-operative factors. Given the Persistence of Force, and given the various derivative laws of Force, and there has to be shown not only how the actual existences of the inorganic world necessarily exhibit the traits they do, but how there necessarily result the more numerous and involved traits exhibited by organic and super-organic existences—how an organism is evolved? what is the genesis of human intelligence? whence social progress arises?

It is evident that this development of Knowledge into an organized aggregate of direct and indirect deductions from the Persistence of Force, can be achieved only in the remote future; and, indeed, cannot be completely achieved even then. Scientific progress is progress in that equilibration of thought and things which we saw is going on, and must continue to go on; but which cannot arrive at perfection in any finite period. Still, though Science can never be entirely reduced to this form; and though only at a far distant time can it be brought nearly to this form; much may even now be done in the way of approximation.

Of course, what may now be done, can be done but very imperfectly by any single individual. No one can possess that encyclopedic information required for rightly organizing even the truths already established. Nevertheless as progress is effected by increments—as all organization, beginning in faint and blurred outlines, is completed by successive modifications and additions; advantage may accrue from an attempt, however rude, to reduce the facts now accumulated—or rather certain classes of them—to something like coordination. Such must be the plea for the several volumes which are to succeed this; dealing with the respective divisions of what we distinguished at the outset as Special Philosophy.

2. Liberalism and the Rights of Children*

After considering such titles as "A System of Social and Political Morality" and "Demostatics," Spencer was persuaded to use "Social Statics" as the title of his first book, published in 1850. The analogy from physics is obvious. Although the term had already been used by Auguste Comte, Spencer disclaimed any knowledge of this; otherwise he would have adhered to his "original title." The book was acclaimed by many journals as "eloquent," "logically-reasoned," "original," etc. But in at least one journal, Eliza Cook's, a critic wrote: "We have heard of the Curiosities of Literature and some day this book will be numbered among them." In any case, Spencer was disappointed at what he felt were "superficial" reviews. In an incredible, but, as Huxley pointed out, characteristically Spencerian performance, Spencer wrote a review of the book himself. Obviously deriving pleasure from stressing his unorthodoxy, he wrote that his doctrines "will horrify many soft-hearted people." And referring to his statement that state interference does more mischief than good when it seeks to ward off "natural" penalties, he added: "Verily this teaching is not meat for babes but for men; and men of strong digestions, too."† Some of the "horrifying" doctrines elab-

* *Social Statics; or The Conditions Essential to Human Happiness Specified, and the First of Them Developed* (New York: D. Appleton and Co., 1873), pp. 93–94; 121–122; 229; 205–213. The subtitles were inserted by the editor.

† *Autobiography*, I, 415–421.

orated in the book were the right to freedom of action,
the right to ignore the state, and the rights of children
to a life based on the same "law of equal freedom" as
that of adults.

THE RIGHT TO FREEDOM OF ACTION

From this conclusion there seems no possibility of escape. Let us repeat the steps by which we arrive at it.
God wills man's happiness. Man's happiness can only be
produced by the exercise of his faculties. Then God
wills that he should exercise his faculties. But to exercise
his faculties he must have liberty to do all that his
faculties naturally impel him to do. Then God intends
he should have that liberty. Therefore he has a right to
that liberty.

This however, is not the right of one but of all. All are
endowed with faculties. All are bound to fulfil the Divine
will by exercising them. All therefore must be free to do
those things in which the exercise of them consists. That
is, all must have rights to liberty of action.

And hence there necessarily arises a limitation. For if
men have like claims to that freedom which is needful
for the exercise of their faculties, then must the freedom
of each be bounded by the similar freedom of all. When,
in the pursuit of their respective ends, two individuals
clash, the movements of the one remain free only in so
far as they do not interfere with the like movements of
the other. This sphere of existence into which we are
thrown not affording room for the unrestrained activity
of all, and yet all possessing in virtue of their constitu-
tions similar claims to such unrestrained activity, there is
no course but to apportion out the unavoidable restraint

equally. Wherefore we arrive at the general proposition, that every man may claim the fullest liberty to exercise his faculties compatible with the possession of like liberty by every other man.

Thus are we brought by several routes to the same conclusion. Whether we reason our way from those fixed conditions under which only the Divine idea—greatest happiness, can be realized—whether we draw our inferences from man's constitution, considering him as a congeries of faculties—or whether we listen to the monitions of a certain mental agency, which seems to have the function of guiding us in this matter, we are alike taught as the law of right social relationships, that—*Every man has freedom to do all that he wills, provided he infringes not the equal freedom of any other man*. Though further qualifications of the liberty of action thus asserted may be necessary, yet we have seen that in the just regulation of a community no further qualifications of it can be recognized. Such further qualifications must ever remain for private and individual application. We must therefore adopt this law of equal freedom in its entirety, as the law on which a correct system of equity is to be based.

THE RIGHT TO IGNORE THE STATE

As a corollary to the proposition that all institutions must be subordinated to the law of equal freedom, we cannot choose but admit the right of the citizen to adopt a condition of voluntary outlawry. If every man has freedom to do all that he wills, provided he infringes not the equal freedom of any other man, then he is free to drop connection with the state—to relinquish its protection, and to refuse paying toward its support. It is self-evident that in so behaving he in no way trenches upon the liberty of others; for his position is a passive one; and whilst passive he cannot become an aggressor. It is equally self-evident that he cannot be compelled to continue one of a political corporation, without a breach of the moral law, seeing that citizenship involves payment of taxes; and the taking away of a man's property against his will, is an infringement of his rights. Government being simply an agent employ in common by a number of individuals to secure to them certain advantages, the very nature of the connection implies that it is for each to say whether he will employ such an agent or not. If any one of them determines to ignore this mutual-safety confederation, nothing can be said except that he loses all claim to its good offices, and exposes himself to the danger of maltreatment—a thing he is quite at liberty to do if he likes. He cannot be coerced into political combination without a breach of the law of equal freedom; he *can* withdraw from it without committing any such breach; and he has therefore a right so to withdraw.

THE RIGHTS OF CHILDREN

If we wish a boy to become a good mechanic, we insure his expertness by an early apprenticeship. The young musician that is to be, passes several hours a day at his instrument. Initiatory courses of outline drawing and shading are gone through by the intended artist. For the future accountant, a thorough drilling in arithmetic is prescribed. The reflective powers are sought to be developed by the study of mathematics. Thus, all training is founded on the principle that culture must precede proficiency. In such proverbs as—"Habit is second nature," and "Practice makes perfect," men have expressed those net products of universal observation on which every educational system is ostensibly based. The maxims of a village schoolmistress and the speculations of a Pestalozzi are alike pervaded by the theory that the child should be accustomed to those exertions of body and mind which will in future life be required of it. Education means this or nothing.

What now is the most important attribute of man as a moral being? What faculty above all others should we be solicitous to cultivate? May we not answer—the faculty of self-control? This it is which forms a chief distinction between the human being and the brute. It is in virtue of this that man is defined as a creature "looking before and after." It is in their larger endowment of this that the civilized races are superior to the savage. In supremacy of this consists one of the perfections of the ideal man. Not to be impulsive—not to be spurred hither and thither by each desire that in turn comes uppermost; but to be self-restrained, self-balanced, governed by the joint decision of the feelings in council assembled, before whom every action shall have been fully debated and calmly determined—this it is which education— moral education at least—strives to produce.

But the power of self-government, like all other powers, can be developed only by exercise. Whoso is to rule over his passions in maturity, must be practised in ruling over his passions during youth. Observe, then, the absurdity of the coercive system. Instead of habituating a boy to be a law to himself as he is required in after-life to be, it administers the law for him. Instead of preparing him against the day when he shall leave the paternal roof, by inducing him to fix the boundaries of his actions and voluntarily confine himself within them, it marks out these boundaries for him, and says—"cross them at your peril." Here we have a being who, in a few years, is to become his own master, and, by way of fitting him for such a condition, he is allowed to be his own master as little as possible. Whilst in every other particular it is thought desirable that what the man will have to do, the child should be well drilled in doing, in this most important of all particulars—the controlling of himself—it is thought that the less practice he has the better. No wonder that those who have been brought up under the severest discipline should so frequently turn out the wildest of the wild. Such a result is just what might have been looked for.

Indeed, not only does the physical-force system fail to fit the youth for his future position; it absolutely tends to unfit him. Were slavery to be his lot—if his after-life had to be passed under the rule of a Russian autocrat, or of an American cotton planter, no better method of training could be devised than one which accustomed him to that attitude of complete subordination he would subsequently have to assume. But just to the degree in which such treatment would fit him for servitude, must it unfit him for being a free man amongst free men.

But why is education needed at all? Why does not the child grow spontaneously into a normal human being? Why should it be requisite to curb this propensity, to stimulate the other sentiment, and thus by artificial aids to mould the mind into something different from what it would of itself become? Is not there here an anomaly in nature? Throughout the rest of creation we find the seed and the embryo attaining to perfect maturity without external aid. Drop an acorn into the ground, and it will in due time become a healthy oak without either pruning or training. The insect passes through its several transformations unhelped, and arrives at its final form possessed of every needful capacity and instinct. No coercion is needed to make the young bird or quadruped adopt the habits proper to its future life. Its character like its body, spontaneously assumes complete fitness for the part it has to play in the world. How happens it, then, that the human mind alone tends to develop itself wrongly? Must there not be some exceptional cause for this? Manifestly: and if so a true theory of education must recognize this cause.

It is an indisputable fact that the moral constitution which fitted man for his original predatory state, differs from the one needed to fit him for this social state to which multiplication of the race has led. In a foregoing part of our inquiry, it was shown that the law of adaptation is effecting a transition from the one constitution to the other. Living then, as we do, in the midst of this transition, we must expect to find sundry phenomena which are explicable only upon the hypothesis that humanity is at present partially adapted to both these states, and not completely to either—has only in a degree lost the dispositions needed for savage life, and has but imperfectly acquired those needed for social life. The anomaly just specified is one of these. The tendency of each new generation to develop itself wrongly, indicates the degree of modification that has yet to take place. Those respects in which a child requires restraint, are just the respects in which he is taking after the aboriginal man. The selfish squabbles of the nursery, the persecution of the play-ground, the lyings and petty thefts, the rough treatment of inferior creatures, the propensity to destroy—all these imply that tendency to pursue gratification at the expense of other beings, which qualified man for the wilderness, and which disqualifies him for civilized life.

We have seen, however, that this incongruity between man's attributes and his conditions is in course of being remedied. We have seen that the instincts of the savage must die of inanition—that the sentiments called forth by the social state must grow by exercise, and that if the laws of life remain constant, this modification will continue until our desires are brought into perfect conformity with our circumstances. When now that ultimate state in which morality shall have become organic is arrived at, this anomaly in the development of the child's character will have disappeared. The young human being will no longer be an exception in nature—will not as now tend to grow into unfitness for the requirements of after-life, but will spontaneously unfold itself into that ideal manhood, whose every impulse coincides with the dictates of the moral law.

Education, therefore, in so far as it seeks to form character, serves only a temporary purpose, and, like other institutions resulting from the non-adaptation of man to the social state, must in the end die out. Hence we see how doubly incongruous with the moral law, is the system of training by coercion. Not only does it necessitate direct violations of that law, but the very work which it so futilely attempts to perform, will not need performing when that law has attained to its final supremacy. Force in the domestic circle, like magisterial force, is merely the complement of immorality: immorality we have found to be resolvable into non-adaptation: non-adaptation must in time cease: and thus the postulate with which this old theory of education starts will eventually become false. Rods and ferules, equally with the staffs and handcuffs of the constable; the gaoler's keys; the swords, bayonets, and cannon, with which nations restrain each other, are the offspring of iniquity—can exist only whilst supported by it, and necessarily share in the badness of their parentage. Born therefore as it is of man's imperfections—governing as it does by means of those imperfections—and abdicating as it must when Equity begins to reign, Coercion in all its forms—education or other—is essentially vicious.

And here we are naturally led to remark once more the necessary incongruity between the perfect law and the imperfect man. Whatsoever of Utopianism there may seem to be in the foregoing doctrines, is due not to any error in them but to faults in ourselves. A partial impracticability must not perplex us; must, on the contrary, be expected. Just in proportion to our distance below the purely moral state, must be our difficulty in acting up to the moral law, either in the treatment of children or in any thing else. It is not for us, however, to magnify and ponder over this difficulty. Our course, is simple. We have just to fulfil the law as far as in us lies, resting satisfied that the limitations necessitated by our present condition will quite soon enough assert themselves.

Meanwhile let it be remarked that the main obstacle to the right conduct of education lies rather in the parent than in the child. It is not that the child is insensible to influences higher than that of force, but that the parent is not virtuous enough to use them. Fathers and mothers who enlarge upon the trouble which filial misbehaviour entails upon them, strangely assume that all the blame is due to the evil propensities of their offspring and none to their own. Though on their knees they confess to being miserable sinners, yet to hear their complaints of undutiful sons and daughters you might suppose that they were themselves immaculate. They forget that the depravity of their children is a reproduction of their own depravity. They do not recognize in these much-scolded, often-beaten little ones, so many looking-glasses wherein they may see reflected their own selfishness. It would astonish them to assert that they behave as improperly to their children as their children do to them. Yet a little candid self-analysis would show them that half their commands are issued more for their own convenience or gratification than for corrective purposes. "I won't have that noise!" exclaims a disturbed father to some group of vociferous juveniles: and the noise ceasing, he claims to have done something toward making his family orderly. Perhaps he has; but how? By exhibiting that same evil disposition which he seeks to check in his children—a determination to sacrifice to his own happiness the happiness of others. Observe, too, the impulse under which a refractory child is punished. Instead of anxiety for the delinquent's welfare, that severe eye and compressed lip denote rather the ire of an offended ruler —express some such inward thought as "You little wretch, we'll soon see who is to be master." Uncover its roots, and the theory of parental authority will be found to grow not out of man's love for his offspring but out of his love of dominion. Let any one who doubts this listen to that common reprimand, "How *dare* you disobey me?" and then consider what the emphasis means. No, no, moral-force education is widely practicable even now, if parents were civilized enough to use it.

But of course the obstacle is in a measure reciprocal. Even the best samples of childhood as we now know it will be occasionally unmanageable by suasion: and when inferior natures have to be dealt with, the difficulty of doing without coercion must be proportionably great.

Nevertheless patience, self-denial, a sufficient insight into youthful emotions, and a due sympathy with them, added to a little ingenuity in the choice of means, will usually accomplish all that can be wished. Only let a parent's actions and words and manner show that his own feeling is a thoroughly right one, and he will rarely fail to awaken a responsive feeling in the breast of his child.

One further objection remains to be noticed. It will probably be said that if the rights of children are coextensive with those of adults, it must follow that children are equally entitled with adults to citizenship, and ought to be similarly endowed with political power. This inference looks somewhat alarming; and it is easy to imagine the triumphant air of those who draw it, and the smiles with which they meditate upon the absurdities it suggests. Nevertheless the answer is simple and decisive. There must go two things to originate an incongruity; and, before passing censure, it is needful say which of the two incongruous things is in fault. In the present case the incongruity is between the institution of government on the one side, and a certain consequence of the law of equal freedom on the other. Which of the two is to be condemned for this? In the above objection it is tacitly assumed that the blame lies with this consequence of the law of equal freedom: whereas the fact is just the other way. It is with the institution of government that the blame lies. Were the institution of government an essentially right one, there would be reason to suppose that our conclusion was fallacious; but being as it is the off-spring of immorality, it must be condemned for conflicting with the moral law, and not the moral law for con-flicting with it. Were the moral law universally obeyed, government would not exist; and did government not exist, the moral law could not dictate the political enfranchisement of children. Hence the alleged absurdity is traceable to the present evil constitution of society, and not to some defect in our conclusion.

Concerning the extension of the law of equal freedom to children, we must therefore say, that equity commands it, and that expediency recommends it. We find the rights of children to be deducible from the same axiom and by the same argument as the rights of adults; whilst denial of them involves us in perplexities out of which there seems to be no escape. The association between filial subservience and barbarism—the evident kinship of filial subservience to social and martial slavery—and the fact that filial subservience declines with the advance of civilization, suggest that such subservience is bad. The viciousness of a coercive treatment of children is further proved by its utter failure to accomplish the chief end of moral education—the culture of the sympathies; by its tendency to excite feelings of antagonism and hate; and by the check which it necessarily puts upon the development of the all-important faculty of self-control. Whilst, on the other hand, a non-coercive treatment being favourable to, and almost necessitating, constant appeals to the higher feelings, must, by exercising those feelings, improve the character; and must, at the same time, accustom the child to that condition of freedom in which its after-life is to be passed. It turns out, too, that the very need for a moral training of children is but temporary and that, consequently, a true theory of the filial relationship must not presuppose like the command-and-obedience theory that such a need is permanent. Lastly, we find reason to attribute whatever of incompatibility there may be between these conclusions and our daily experience, not to any error in them, but to the necessary incongruity between the perfect law and an imperfect humanity.

3. National Education*

In "National Education," one chapter of Social Statics, *Spencer elaborated for the first time on the social and political aspects of education, which he regarded as integral parts of his broader social ideology. His views on the educational role of the state were "deduced" from the "law of equal freedom." The chapter on education, his biographer wrote, "was a theme of controversy from the beginning." On the one hand, the Congregational Board of Education saw fit to reprint it under the title "State Education Self-Defeating" (1851) in order to bolster their Nonconformist interests; and as late as 1902, the Northumberland Society for the Liberation of Education from State Control reprinted it to promote their own interests. On the other hand, Spencer wrote, "the National Public School Association are falling foul of me."†*

1. In the same way that our definition of state-duty forbids the state to administer religion or charity, so likewise does it forbid the state to administer education. Inasmuch as the taking away, by government, of more of a man's property than is needful for maintaining his rights, is an infringement of his rights, and therefore a reversal of the government's function toward him; and inasmuch

* Social Statics; or The Conditions Essential to Human Happiness Specified, and the First of Them Developed (New York: D. Appleton and Co., 1873), pp. 360–390. Abridged.
† Life and Letters, I, 78; II, 212.

as the taking away of his property to educate his own or other people's children is not needful for the maintaining of his rights; the taking away of his property for such a purpose is wrong.

Should it be said that the rights of the children are involved, and that state-interposition is required to maintain these, the reply is that no cause for such interposition can be shown until the children's rights have been violated, and that their rights are not violated by a neglect of their education. For, as repeatedly explained, what we call rights are merely arbitrary subdivisions of the general liberty to exercise the faculties; and that only can be called an infringement of rights which actually diminishes this liberty—cuts off a previously existing power to pursue the objects of desire. Now the parent who is careless of a child's education does not do this. The liberty to exercise the faculties is left intact. Omitting instruction in no way takes from a child's freedom to do whatsoever it wills in the best way it can; and this freedom is all that equity demands. Every aggression, be it remembered—every infraction of rights, is necessarily *active;* whilst every neglect, carelessness, omission, is as necessarily *passive.* Consequently, however wrong the non-performance of a parental duty may be—however much it is condemned by that secondary morality—the morality of beneficence—it does not amount to a breach of the law of equal freedom, and cannot therefore be taken cognizance of by the state.

2.   Were there no direct disproof of the frequently alleged right to education at the hands of the state, the absurdities in which it entangles its assertors would sufficiently show its invalidity. Conceding for a moment that the government is bound to educate a man's children, then, what kind of logic will demonstrate that it is not

bound to feed and clothe them? If there should be an act-of-parliament provision for the development of their minds, why should there not be an act-of-parliament provision for the development of their bodies? If the mental wants of the rising generation ought to be satisfied by the state, why not their physical ones? The reasoning which is held to establish the right to intellectual food, will equally well establish the right to material food: nay, will do more—will prove that children should be altogether cared for by government. For if the benefit, importance, or necessity of education be assigned as a sufficient reason why government should educate, then may the benefit, importance, or necessity of food, clothing, shelter, and warmth be assigned as a sufficient reason why government should administer these also. So that the alleged right cannot be established without annulling all parental responsibility whatever.

Should further refutation be thought needful, there is the ordeal of a definition. We lately found this ordeal fatal to the assumed right to a maintenance; we shall find it equally fatal to this assumed right to education. For what is an education? Where, between the teaching of a dame-school, and the most comprehensive university *curriculum,* can be drawn the line separating that portion of mental culture which may be justly claimed of the state, from that which may not be so claimed? What peculiar quality is there in reading, writing, and arithmetic, which gives the embryo citizen a right to have them imparted to him, but which quality is not shared in by geography, and history, and drawing, and the natural sciences? Must calculation be taught because it is useful? why so is geometry, as the carpenter and mason will tell us; so is chemistry, as we may gather from dyers and bleachers; so is physiology, as is abundantly proved by the ill-health written in so many faces. Astronomy, mechanics, geology, and the various connate sciences—should not these be taught, too? they are all useful. Where is the unit of measure by which we may determine the respective values of different kinds of knowledge? Or, assuming them determined, how can it be shown that a child may claim from the civil power knowledge of such and such values, but not knowledge of certain less values? When those who demand a state-education can say exactly how much is due—can agree upon what the young have a right to, and what not—it will be time to listen. But until they accomplish this impossibility, their plea cannot be entertained.

3. A sad snare would these advocates of legislative teaching betray themselves into, could they substantiate their doctrine. For what is meant by saying that a government ought to educate the people? why should they be educated? what is the education for? Clearly to fit the people for social life—to make them good citizens. And who is to say what are good citizens? The government: there is no other judge. And who is to say how these good citizens may be made? The government: there is no other judge. Hence the proposition is convertible into this—a government ought to mould children into good citizens, using its own discretion in settling what a good citizen is, and how the child may be moulded into one. It must first form for itself a definite conception of a pattern citizen; and having done this, must elaborate such system of discipline as seems best calculated to produce citizens after that pattern. This system of discipline it is bound to enforce to the uttermost. For if it does otherwise, it allows men to become different from what in its judgment they should become, and therefore fails in that duty it is charged to fulfil. Being thus justified in carrying

out rigidly such plans as it thinks best, every government ought to do what the despotic governments of the Continent and of China do.

Now a minute dictation like this, which extends to every action, and will brook no nay, is the legitimate realization of this state-education theory. Whether the government has got erroneous conceptions of what citizens ought to be, or whether the methods of training it adopts are injudicious, is not the question. According to the hypothesis it is commissioned to discharge a specified function. It finds no ready-prescribed way of doing this. It has no alternative, therefore, but to choose that way which seems to it most fit. And as there exists no higher authority, either to dispute or confirm its judgment, it is justified in the absolute enforcement of its plans, be they what they may. As from the proposition that government ought to teach religion, there springs the other proposition, that government must decide what is religious truth, and how it is to be taught; so, the assertion that government ought to educate, necessitates the further assertion that it must say what education is, and how it shall be conducted. And the same rigid popery, which we found to be a logical consequence in the one case, follows in the other also.

.   .   .

5. But it is argued that parents, and especially those whose children most need instructing, do not know what good instruction is. "In the matter of education," says Mr. Mill, "the intervention of government is justifiable; because the case is one in which the interest and judgment of the consumer are not sufficient security for the goodness of the commodity."

It is strange that so judicious a writer should feel satisfied with such a worn-out excuse. This alleged incompetency on the part of the people has been the reason assigned for all state-interferences whatever.

Should it be said that the propriety of legislative control depends upon circumstances; that respecting some articles the judgment of the consumer *is* sufficient, whilst respecting other articles it is not; and that the difficulty of deciding upon its quality, places education amongst these last; the reply again is, that the same has been said on behalf of all meddlings in turn. Plenty of trickeries, plenty of difficulties in the detection of fraud, plenty of instances showing the inability of purchasers to protect themselves, are quoted by the advocates of each proposed recourse to official regulation; and in each case it is urged that here, at any rate, official regulation is required. Yet does experience disprove these inferences one after another, teaching us that, in the long run, the interest of the consumer is not only an efficient guarantee for the goodness of the things consumed, but the best guarantee. Is it not unwise, then, to trust for the hundredth time in one of these plausible but deceptive conclusions? Is it not rational, rather, to infer, that however much appearances are to the contrary, the choice of the commodity—education, like the choice of all other commodities, may be safely left to the discretion of buyers?

Still more reasonable will this inference appear on observing that the people are not, after all, such incompetent judges of education as they seem. Ignorant parents are generally quick enough to discern the effects of good or bad teaching; will note them in the children of others, and act accordingly. Moreover it is easy for them to follow the example of the better instructed, and choose the same schools. Or they may get over the difficulty by asking advice; and there is generally some one both able and willing to give the uneducated parent a trustworthy answer to his inquiry about teachers. Lastly, there is the test of price. With education, as with other things, price is a tolerably safe index of value; it is one open to all classes; and it is one which the poor instinctively appeal to in the matter of schools; for it is notorious that they look coldly at very cheap or gratuitous instruction.

But even admitting that, whilst this defect of judgment is not virtually so extreme as is alleged, it is nevertheless great, the need for interference is still denied. The evil is undergoing rectification, as all analogous ones are or have been. The rising generation will better understand what good education is than their parents do, and their descendants will have clearer conceptions of it still. Whoso thinks the slowness of the process a sufficient reason for meddling, must, to be consistent, meddle in all other things; for the ignorance which in every case serves as an excuse for state-interposition is of very gradual cure. The errors both of consumers and producers often take generations to set right. Improvements in the carrying on of commerce, in manufactures, and especially in agriculture, spread almost imperceptibly. Take rotation of crops for an example. And if this tardiness is a valid argument for interference in one case, why not in others? Why not have farms superintended by government, because it may take a century for farmers generally to adopt the plans suggested by modern science?

Did we duly realize the fact that society is a growth, and not a manufacture—a thing that makes itself, and not a thing that can be artificially made—we should fall into fewer mistakes; and we should see that amongst other imperfections this incompetence of the masses to distinguish good instruction from bad, is being outgrown.

6. When in the matter of education "the interest and

judgment of the consumer" are said not to be "sufficient security for the goodness of the commodity," and when it is argued that government superintendence is therefore needful, a very questionable assumption is made: the assumption, namely, that "the interest and judgment" of a government *are* sufficient security. Now there is good reason to dispute this, nay, even to assert that, taking the future into account, they offer much less security.

The problem is, how best to develop minds: a problem amongst the most difficult—may we not say, *the* most difficult? Two things are needful for its solution. First, to know what minds should be fashioned into. Next, to know how they may be so fashioned. From the work to be done, turn we now to the proposed doers of it. Men of education (as the word goes) they no doubt are; well-meaning, many of them; thoughtful, some; philosophical, a few; men, however, for the most part, born with silver spoons in their mouths, and prone to regard human affairs as reflected in these—somewhat distortedly. Very comfortable lives are led by the majority of them, and hence "things as they are" find favour in their eyes. For their tastes—they are shown in the subordination of national business to the shooting of grouse and the chasing of foxes. For their pride—it is in wide estates or long pedigrees; and should the family coat of arms bear some such ancient motto as "Strike hard," or, "Furth fortune, and fill the fetters," it is a great happiness. As to their ideal of society, it is either a sentimental feudalism; or it is a state, something like the present, under which the people shall be respectful to their betters, and "content with that station of life to which it has pleased God to call them;" or it is state arranged with the view of making each labourer the most efficient producing tool, to the end that the accumulation of wealth may be the greatest possible. Add to this, that their notions of moral discipline are shown in the maintenance of capital punishment, and in the sending of their sons to schools where flogging is practised, and where they themselves were brought up. Now could the judgment of such respecting the commodity—education, be safely relied on? Certainly not.

Still less might their "interest" be trusted. Though at variance with that of the people, it would inevitably be followed in preference. The self-seeking which, consciously or unconsciously, sways rulers in other cases, would sway them in this likewise—could not fail to do so, whilst the character of men is what it is. With taxation unequally distributed, with such a glaringly unjust apportionment of representatives to population, with a nepotism that fills lucrative places with Greys and Elliots, with a staff of a hundred animals more than are wanted, with lavish pensions to the undeserving, with a system of retrenchment which discharges common men and retains officers, and with such votes as those given by the military, the naval, the landed, and the clerically-related members of parliament, we may be quite sure that a state-education would be administered for the advantage of those in power, rather than for the advantage of the nation. To hope for any thing else is to fall into the old error of looking for grapes from thorns. Nothing can be more truly Utopian than expecting that, with men and things as they are, the influences which have vitiated all other institutions would not vitiate this one.

Thus, even were it true that in the matter of education "the interest and judgment of the consumer are not sufficient security for the goodness of the commodity," the wisdom of superseding them by the "interest and judgment" of a government is by no means obvious. It may, indeed, be said that the argument proves only the unfitness of existing governments to become national teachers, and not the unfitness of a government normally constituted: whereas the object of inquiry being to determine what a government *should* do, the hypothesis must be that the government is what it *should* be. To this the reply is, that the nature of the allegation to be met necessitates a descent to the level of present circumstances. It is on the defective "interest and judgment" of the people, *as they now are,* that the plea for legislative superintendence is based; and, consequently, in criticizing this plea we must take government *as it now is.* We cannot reason as though government were what it should be; since, before it can become so, any alleged deficiency of "interest and judgment" on the part of the people must have disappeared.

7. The impolicy of setting up a national organization for cultivating the popular mind, and commissioning the government to superintend this organization, is further seen in the general truth that every such organization is in spirit conservative, and not progressive. All institutions have an instinct of self-preservation growing out of the selfishness of those connected with them. Being dependent for their vitality upon the continuance of existing arrangements, they naturally uphold these. Their roots are in the past and the present; never in the future. Change threatens them, modifies them, eventually destroys them; hence to change they are uniformly opposed. On the other hand, education, properly so called, is closely associated with change—is its pioneer—is the never-sleeping agent of revolution—is always fitting men for higher things, and *un*fitting them for things as they are. Therefore, between institutions whose very existence depends upon man continuing what he is, and

true education, which is one of the instruments for making him something other than he is, there must always be enmity.

Still more manifest becomes this obstructive tendency on considering that the very organizations devised for the spreading of knowledge, may themselves act as suppressors of it. Thus it is said, that Oxford was one of the last places in which the Newtonian philosophy was acknowledged. We read again, in the life of Locke, that "there was a meeting of the heads of houses at Oxford, where it was proposed to censure and discourage the reading of this essay (On the Human Understanding); and after various debates, it was concluded that without any public censure each head of a house shall endeavour to prevent its being read in his own college." At Eton, too, in Shelley's time, "Chemistry was a forbidden thing," even to the banishment of chemical treatises. So uniformly has it been the habit of these endowed institutions to close the door against innovations, that they are amongst the last places to which any one looks for improvements in the art of teaching, or a better choice of subjects to be taught. The attitude of the universities toward natural science has been that of contemptuous non-recognition. College authorities have long resisted, either actively or passively, the making of physiology, chemistry, geology, &c., subjects of examination; and only of late, under pressure from with, and under the fear of being supplanted by rival institutions, have new studies been gingerly taken to.

Now, although *vis inertiæ* may be very useful in its place—although the resistance of office-holders has its function—although we must not quarrel with this instinct of self-preservation which gives to institutions their vitality, because it also upholds them through a lingering decrepitude—we may yet wisely refuse to increase its natural effect. It is very necessary to have in our social economy a conservative force as well as a reforming one, that there may be progress for the *resultant;* but it is highly impolitic to afford the one an artificial advantage over the other. To establish a state-education is to do this, however. The teaching organization itself, and the government which directs it, will inevitably lean to things as they are; and to give them control over the national mind, is to give them the means of repressing aspirations after things as they should be. Just that culture which seems compatible with their own preservation will these institutions allow, whilst just that culture which, by advancing society, threatens to sap their own foundations, or, in other words—just that culture which is most valuable, they will oppose.

The sanguine will perhaps hope that, though this has been the rule hitherto, it will not be the rule in future. Let them not deceive themselves. So long as men pursue private advantage at the expense of the common weal, that is to say—so long as government is needful at all, so long will this be true. Less marked the tendency will no doubt be in proportion as men are less unjustly selfish. But to whatever extent they lack perfect conscientiousness, to the same extent will vested interests sway them, and to the same extent will institutions resist change.

8. . . . Somewhat like this childish impatience is the feeling exhibited by not a few state-educationists. Both they and their type show a lack of faith in natural forces —almost an ignorance that there are such forces. In both there is the same dissatisfaction with the ordained rate of progress. And by both, artificial means are used to remedy what are conceived to be nature's failures. Within these few years men have all at once been awakened to the importance of instructing the people. That to which they were awhile since indifferent or even hostile has sud-

denly become an object of enthusiasm. With all the ardour of recent converts—with all a novice's inordinate expectations—with all the eagerness of a lately-aroused desire—do they await the hoped-for result; and, with the unreasonableness ever attendant upon such a state of mind, are dissatisfied, because the progress from general ignorance to universal enlightenment has not been completed in a generation. One would have thought it sufficiently clear to everybody that the great changes taking place in this world of ours are uniformly slow. Continents are upheaved at the rate of a foot or two in a century. The deposition of a delta is the work of tens of thousands of years. The transformation of barren rock into life-supporting soil takes countless ages. If any think society advances under a different law, let them read. Has it not required the whole Christian era to abolish slavery in Europe? as far at least as it is abolished. Did not a hundred generations live and die while picture-writing grew into printing? Have not science and commerce and mechanical skill increased at a similarly tardy pace? Yet are men disappointed that a pitiful fifty years has not sufficed for thorough popular enlightenment! Although within this period an advance has been made far beyond what the calm thinker would have expected—far beyond what the past rate of progress in human affairs seemed to prophesy—yet do these so impatient people summarily condemn the voluntary system as a failure! A natural process—a process spontaneously set up—a process of self-unfolding which the national mind had commenced, is pooh-poohed because it has not wrought a total transformation in the course of what constitutes but a day in the life of humanity! And then, to make up for nature's incompetency, the unfolding must be hastened by legislative fingerings!

9.   There is, indeed, one excuse for attempts to spread

education by artificial means, namely, the anxiety to diminish crime, of which education is supposed to be a preventive. "We hold," says Mr. Macaulay, "that whoever has the right to hang has the right to educate."* And in a letter relative to the Manchester district-system, Miss Martineau writes—"Nor can I see that political economy objects to the general rating for educational purposes. As a mere police-tax this rating would be a very cheap affair. It would cost us much less than we now pay for juvenile depravity." In both which remarks this prevalent belief is implied.

Now, with all respect to the many high authorities holding it, the truth of this belief may be disputed. We have no evidence that education, as commonly understood, is a preventive of crime. Those perpetually reiterated newspaper paragraphs, in which the ratios of instructed to uninstructed convicts are so triumphantly stated, prove just nothing. Before any inference can be drawn, it must be shown that these instructed and uninstructed convicts, come from two *equal* sections of society, alike *in all other respects* but that of knowledge— similar in rank and occupation, having similar advantages, labouring under similar temptations. But this is not only not the truth; it is nothing like the truth. The many ignorant criminals belong to a most unfavourably circumstanced class; whilst the few educated ones are from a class comparatively favoured. As things stand it would be equally logical to infer that crime arises from going without animal food, or from living in badly-ventilated rooms, or from wearing dirty shirts; for were the inmates of a gaol to be catechized, it would doubtless be found that the majority of them had been placed in these conditions. Ignorance and crime are not cause and

* Quoted from a speech at Edinburgh.

effect; they are coincident results of the same cause. To be wholly untaught is to have moved amongst those whose incentives to wrong-doing are strongest; to be partially taught is to have been one of a class subject to less urgent temptations; to be well taught is to have lived almost beyond the reach of the usual motives for transgression. Ignorance, therefore (at least in the statistics referred to), simply indicates the presence of crime-producing influences, and can no more be called the cause of crime than the falling of a barometer can be called the cause of rain.

The fact is, that scarcely any connection exists between morality and the discipline of ordinary teaching. Mere culture of the intellect (and education as usually conducted amounts to little more) is hardly at all operative upon conduct. Creeds pasted upon the memory, good principles learnt by rote, lessons in right and wrong, will not eradicate vicious propensities, though people, in spite of their experience as parents, and as citizens, persist in hoping they will. All history, both of the race and of individuals, goes to prove that in the majority of cases precepts do not act at all. And where they seem to act, it is not by them, but by preëxisting feelings which respond to them, that the effects are really produced. Intellect is not a power, but an instrument—not a thing which itself moves and works, but a thing which is moved and worked by forces behind it. To say that men are ruled by reason, is as irrational as to say that men are ruled by their eyes. Reason *is* an eye—the eye through which the desires see their way to gratification. And educating it only makes it a better eye—gives it a vision more accurate and more comprehensive—does not at all alter the desires subserved by it. However far seeing you make it, the passions will still determine the directions in which it shall be turned—the objects on which it shall dwell. Just those ends which the instincts or sentiments propose will the intellect be employed to accomplish: culture of it having done nothing but increase the ability to accomplish them. Probably some will urge that enlightening men enables them to discern the penalties which naturally attach to wrong-doing; and in a certain sense this is true. But it is only superficially true. Though they may learn that the grosser crimes commonly bring retribution in one shape or other, they will not learn that the subtler ones do. Their sins will merely be made more Machiavellian.

There is, in fact, a quite sufficient reason for failure—no less a reason than the impossibility of the task. The expectation that crime may presently be cured, whether by state-education, or the silent system, or the separate system, or any other system, is one of those Utopianisms fallen into by people who pride themselves on being practical. Crime is incurable, save by that gradual process of adaptation to the social state which humanity is undergoing. Crime is the continual breaking out of the old unadapted nature—the index of a character unfitted to its conditions—and only as fast as the unfitness diminishes can crime diminish. To hope for some prompt method of putting down crime, is in reality to hope for some prompt method of putting down all evils—laws, governments, taxation, poverty, caste, and the rest; for they and crime have the same root. Reforming men's conduct without reforming their natures is impossible; and to expect that their natures may be reformed, otherwise than by the forces which are slowly civilizing us, is visionary. Schemes of discipline or culture are of use only in proportion as they organically alter the national character, and the extent to which they do this is by no means great. It is not by humanly-devised agencies, good as these may be in their way, but it is by the never-ceasing action of circumstances upon men—by the constant pressure of their new conditions upon them—that the required change is mainly effected.

Meanwhile it may be remarked, that whatever moral benefit *can* be effected by education, must be effected by an education which is emotional rather than perceptive. If, in place of making a child *understand* that this thing is right and the other wrong, you make it *feel* that they are so—if you make virtue *loved* and vice *loathed*— if you arouse a noble *desire*, and make torpid an inferior one—if you bring into life a previously dormant *sentiment*—if you cause a sympathetic *impulse* to get the better of one that is selfish—if, in short, you produce a state of mind to which proper behaviour is *natural, spontaneous, instinctive*, you do some good. But no drilling in catechisms, no teaching of moral codes, can effect this. Only by repeatedly awakening the appropriate *emotions* can character be changed. Mere ideas received by the intellect, meeting no response from within—having no roots there—are quite inoperative upon conduct, and are quickly forgotten upon entering into life.

Perhaps it will be said that a discipline like this now described as the only efficient one, might be undertaken by the state. No doubt it might. But from all legislative attempts at emotional education may Heaven defend us!

10. Yet another objection remains. Just as we found, on close examination, by poor-laws a government cannot really cure distress, but can only shift it from one section of the community to another, so, astounding as the assertion looks, we shall find that a government cannot in fact educate at all, but can only educate some by *un*educating others. If, before agitating the matter, men

had taken the precaution to define education, they would probably have seen that the state can afford no true help in the matter. But having unfortunately neglected to do this, they have confined their attention solely to the education given at school, and have forgotten to inquire how their plans bear upon the education which commences when school-days end. It is not indeed that they do not know this discipline of daily duty to be valuable —more valuable, in fact, than the discipline of the teacher. You may often hear them remark as much. But, with the eagerness usual amongst schemers, they are so absorbed in studying the *action* of their proposed mechanism as to overlook its *reaction*.

Now of all qualities which is the one men most need? To the absence of what quality are popular distresses mainly attributable? What is the quality in which the improvident masses are so deficient? Self-restraint—the ability to sacrifice a small present gratification for a prospective great one. A labourer endowed with due self-restraint would never spend his Saturday-night's wages at the public-house. Had he enough self-restraint, the artisan would not live up to his income during prosperous times and leave the future unprovided for. More self-restraint would prevent imprudent marriages and the growth of a pauper population. And were there no drunkenness, no extravagance, no reckless multiplication, social miseries would be trivial.

Consider next how the power of self-restraint is to be increased. By a sharp experience alone can any thing be done. Those in whom this faculty needs drawing out— *educating* must be left to the discipline of nature, and allowed to bear the pains attendant on their defect of character. The only cure for imprudence is the suffering which imprudence entails. Nothing but bringing him face to face with stern necessity, and letting him feel how unbending, how unpitying, are her laws, can improve the man of ill-governed desires. As already shown all interposing between humanity and the conditions of its existence—cushioning-off consequences by poor-laws or the like—serves but to neutralize the remedy and prolong the evil. Let us never forget that the law is—adaptation to circumstances, be they what they may. And if, rather than allow men to come in contact with the real circumstances of their position, we place them in artificial—in false circumstances, they will adapt themselves to these instead; and will, in the end, have to undergo the miseries of a readaptation to the real ones.

11. Thus, in the present, as in other cases, we find the dictate of the abstract law enforced by secondary considerations. The alleged right to education at the hands of the state proves to be untenable; first, as logically committing its supporters to other claims too absurd for consideration; and again, as being incapable of definition. Moreover, could the claim be established, it would imply the duty of government despotically to enforce its system of discipline, and the duty of the subject to submit. That education ought not to be dealt in after the same manner as other things, because in its case "the interest and judgment of the consumer are not sufficient security for the goodness of the commodity," is a plea with most suspicious antecedents; having been many times employed in other instances, and many times disproved. Neither is the implied assumption that the "interest and judgment" of a government *would* constitute a sufficient security admissible. On the contrary, experience proves that the interests of a government, and of all the institutions it may set up, are directly opposed to education of the most important kind. Again, to say that legis-

lative teaching is needful, because other teaching has failed, presupposes a pitiably narrow view of human progress; and further, involves the strange scepticism that, though natural agencies have brought the enlightenment of mankind to its present height, and are even now increasing it at an unparalleled rate, they will no longer answer. The belief that education is a preventive of crime, having no foundation either in theory or fact, cannot be held an excuse for interference. And, to crown all, it turns out that the institution so much longed for is a mere dead machine, which can only give out in one form the power it absorbs in another, minus the friction—a thing which cannot stir toward effecting this kind of education without abstracting the force now accomplishing that—a thing, therefore, which cannot educate at all.

4.   Political Education*

*In his article, "Parliamentary Reform: Its Dangers, and
the Safeguards," first published in the* Westminster Review *in 1860, Spencer dealt with his favorite topic,
namely the dangers of "over-legislation," and with the
related topic of the locus of political power (upper
classes, working classes, artisans, etc.). Political power as
had hitherto been exercised by certain classes—mostly
middle and upper—had been considerably "abused," according to Spencer, and there was no guarantee that
abuses would not continue if such power were placed in
the hands of other classes. The only safeguards against
possible abuses of power by any politically dominant
group, Spencer indicated, was "the spread of sounder
views," and "the moral advance which such sounder
views imply." In short, "the people must be educated."
But Spencer rejected greater amounts of the existing type
of education as not necessarily leading to sound political
participation. Instead, he called for "political knowledge," or "knowledge of Social Science." Spencer's answer
may be debatable as the practices which he criticized;
yet he raised a very fundamental question which modern
polities, especially liberal democracies, have not been
able to answer satisfactorily: What is the most suitable*

* Essays: Scientific, Political, and Speculative (New York: D.
Appleton and Co., 1864), Vol. II, pp. 244–249. This part of the
essay formed the major portion of another article, "On Political
Education," included in The Culture Demanded by Modern Life,
edited by E. L. Youmans (New York: D. Appleton and Co., 1867).

type of education for the "political socialization" of the individual?

Yes, education is the thing wanted; but not the education for which most men agitate. Ordinary school-training is not a preparation for the right exercise of political power. Conclusive proof of this is given by the fact that the artizans, from whose mistaken ideas the most danger is to be feared, are the best informed of the working classes. Far from promising to be a safeguard, the spread of such education as is commonly given, appears more likely to increase the danger. Raising the working classes in general to the artizan-level of culture, rather threatens to augment their power of working political evil. The current faith in Reading, Writing, and Arithmetic, as fitting men for citizenship, seems to us quite unwarranted: as are, indeed, most other anticipations of the benefits to be derived from learning lessons. There is no connexion between the ability to parse a sentence, and a clear understanding of the causes that determine the rate of wages. The multiplication-table affords no aid in seeing through the fallacy that the destruction of property is good for trade. Long practice may have produced extremely good penmanship without having given the least power to understand the paradox, that machinery eventually increases the number of persons employed in the trades into which it is introduced. Nor is it proved that smatterings of mensuration, astronomy, or geography, fit men for estimating the characters and motives of Parliamentary candidates. Indeed we have only thus to bring together the antecedents and the anticipated consequents, to see how untenable is the belief in a relation between them. When we wish a girl to become a good musician, we seat her before the piano: we do not put drawing implements into her hands, and expect music to come along with the skill in the use of pencils and colour-brushes. Sending a boy to pore over law-books, would be thought an extremely irrational way of preparing him for civil engineering. And if in these and all other cases, we do not expect fitness for any function except through instruction and exercise in that function; why do we expect fitness for citizenship to be produced by a discipline which has no relation to the duties of the citizen? Probably it will be replied that by making the working man a good reader, we give him access to sources of information from which he may learn how to use his electoral power; and that other studies sharpen his faculties and make him a better judge of political questions. This is true; and the eventual tendency is unquestionably good. But what if for a long time to come he reads only to obtain confirmation of his errors? What if there exists a literature appealing to his prejudices, and supplying him with fallacious arguments for the mistaken beliefs which he naturally takes up? What if he rejects all teaching that aims to disabuse him of cherished delusion? Must we not say that the culture which thus merely helps the workman to establish himself in error, rather unfits than fits him for citizenship? And do not the trades'-unions furnish us with evidence of this?

How little that which people commonly call education prepares them for the use of political power, may be judged from the incompetency of those who have received the highest education the country affords. Glance back at the blunders of our legislation, and then remember that the men who committed them had mostly taken University-degrees; and you must admit that the profoundest ignorance of Social Science may accompany intimate acquaintance with all that our cultivated classes regard as valuable knowledge. Do but take a young member of Parliament, fresh from Oxford or Cambridge and ask him what he thinks Law should do, and why? or what it should not do, and why? and it will become manifest that neither his familiarity with Aristotle nor his readings in Thucydides, have prepared him to answer the very first question a legislator ought to solve. A single illustration will suffice to show how different an education from that usually given, is required by legislators, and consequently by those who elect them: we mean the illustration which the Free-trade agitation supplies. By kings, peers, and members of Parliament, mostly brought up at universities, trade had been hampered by protections, prohibitions, and bounties. For centuries had been maintained these legislative appliances which a very moderate insight shows to be detrimental. Yet, of all the highly-educated throughout the nation during these centuries, scarcely a man saw how mischievous such appliances were. Not from one who devoted himself to the most approved studies, came the work which set politicians right on these points; but from one who left college without a degree, and prosecuted inquiries which the established education ignored. Adam Smith examined for himself the industrial phenomena of societies; contemplated the productive and distributive activities going on around him; traced out their complicated mutual dependences; and thus reached general principles for political guidance. In recent days, those who have most clearly understood the truths he enunciated, and by persevering exposition have converted the nation to their views, have not been graduates of universities. While, contrariwise, those who have passed through the prescribed *curriculum*, have commonly been the most bitter and obstinate opponents of the changes dictated by politico-economical science. In this all-important direction, right legislation was urged by men deficient in the so-called best education; and was resisted by the great majority of men who had received this so-called best education!

The truth for which we contend, and which is so strangely overlooked, is, indeed, almost a truism. Does not our whole theory of training imply that the right preparation for political power is political cultivation? Must not that teaching which can alone guide the citizen in the fulfillment of his public actions, be a teaching that acquaints him with the effects of public actions?

The second chief safeguard to which we must trust is, then, the spread, not of that mere technical and miscellaneous knowledge which men are so eagerly propagating, but of political knowledge; or, to speak more accurately—knowledge of Social Science. Above all, the essential thing is, the establishment of a true theory of government—a true conception of what legislation is for, and what are its proper limits. This question which our political discussions habitually ignore, is a question of greater moment than any other. Inquiries which statesmen deride as speculative and unpractical, will one day be found infinitely more practical than those which they wade through Blue Books to master, and nightly spend many hours in debating. The considerations that every morning fill a dozen columns of *The Times*, are mere frivolities when compared with the fundamental consideration—What is the proper sphere of government? Before discussing the way in which law should regulate some particular thing, would it not be wise to put the previous question—Whether law ought or ought not to meddle with that thing? and before answering this, to put the more general question—What law should do, and what it should leave undone? Surely, if there are any limits at all to legislation, the settlement of these limits must have effects far more profound than any particular Act of Parliament can have; and must be by so much the more momentous. Surely, if there is danger that the people may misuse political power, it is of supreme importance that they should be taught for what purpose political power ought alone to be used.

Did the upper classes understand their position, they would, we think, see that the diffusion of sound views on this matter more nearly concerns their own welfare and that of the nation at large, than any other thing whatever. Popular influence will inevitably go on increasing. Should the masses gain a predominant power while their ideas of social arrangements and legislative action remain as crude as at present, there will certainly result disastrous meddlings with the relations of capital and labour, as well as a disastrous extension of State-administrations. Immense damage will be inflicted: primarily on employers; secondarily on the employed; and eventually on the nation as a whole. These evils can be prevented, only by establishing in the public mind, a profound conviction that there are certain comparatively narrow limits to the functions of the State; and that these limits ought on no account to be transgressed. Having first learned what these limits are, the upper classes ought energetically to use all means of teaching them to the people.

II

Science, Culture,
and the Arts

5.   What Knowledge Is of Most Worth?*

*The most famous and the most often quoted of Spencer's
educational essays, "What Knowledge Is of Most
Worth?" was ostensibly a review of a series of lectures on
the importance of science in education, delivered at the
Royal Institution in 1854 and published in book form in
1855. "When this essay was written," Spencer later recalled, "its leading thesis, that the teaching of the classics
should give place to the teaching of science, was regarded
by nine out of ten cultivated people as simply mon-
strous." Although not directly bearing upon the doctrine
of evolution, which he developed more fully after the
essay was published, its emphasis on "comprehensive
scientific culture" was, according to Spencer, "an insistence on the acquisition of that knowledge from which
the doctrine of evolution is an eventual outcome."†*

This article first appeared in 1859 in the Westminster
Review. *It was then included as the first chapter of* Education: Intellectual, Moral and Physical, *published in
the United States by D. Appleton and Company in 1860
and in England by G. Manwaring in 1861. Subsequently,
this volume went through numerous editions in both
countries.*

Thoroughly to realise the truth that with the mind as

* *Essays on Education, Etc.* (London: J. M. Dent and Sons, Ltd.,
1911), pp. 3–44. Abridged.
† *Autobiography,* II, 42–44.

with the body the ornamental precedes the useful, it is requisite to glance at its rationale. This lies in the fact that, from the far past down even to the present, social needs have subordinated individual needs, and that the chief social need has been the control of individuals. It is not, as we commonly suppose, that there are no governments but those of monarchs, and parliaments, and constituted authorities. These acknowledged governments are supplemented by other unacknowledged ones, that grow up in all circles, in which every man or woman strives to be king or queen or lesser dignitary. To get above some and be reverenced by them, and to propitiate those who are above us, is the universal struggle in which the chief energies of life are expended. By the accumulation of wealth, by style of living, by beauty of dress, by display of knowledge or intellect, each tries to subjugate others; and so aids in weaving that ramified network of restraints by which society is kept in order. It is not the savage chief only, who, in formidable war-paint, with scalps at his belt, aims to strike awe into his inferiors; it is not only the belle who, by elaborate toilet, polished manners, and numerous accomplishments, strives to "make conquests;" but the scholar, the historian, the philosopher, use their acquirements to the same end. We are none of us content with quietly unfolding our own individualities to the full in all directions; but have a restless craving to impress our individualities upon others, and in some way subordinate them. And this it is which determines the character of our education. Not what knowledge is of most real worth, is the consideration; but what will bring most applause, honour, respect—what will most conduce to social position and influence—what will be most imposing. As, throughout life, not what we are, but what we shall be thought, is the question; so in education, the question is, not the intrinsic value of knowledge, so much as its extrinsic effects on others. And this being our dominant idea, direct utility is scarcely more regarded than by the barbarian when filing his teeth and staining his nails.

If there requires further evidence of the rude, undeveloped character of our education, we have it in the fact that the comparative worths of different kinds of knowledge have been as yet scarcely even discussed—much less discussed in a methodic way with definite results. Not only is it that no standard of relative values has yet been agreed upon; but the existence of any such standard has not been conceived in a clear manner. And not only is it that the existence of such a standard has not been clearly conceived; but the need for it seems to have been scarcely even felt. Men read books on this topic, and attend lectures on that; decide that their children shall be instructed in these branches of knowledge, and shall not be instructed in those; and all under the guidance of mere custom, or liking, or prejudice; without ever considering the enormous importance of determining in some rational way what things are really most worth learning. It is true that in all circles we hear occasional remarks on the importance of this or the other order of information. But whether the degree of its importance justifies the expenditure of the time needed to acquire it; and whether there are not things of more importance to which such time might be better devoted; are queries which, if raised at all, are disposed of quite summarily, according to personal predilections. It is true also, that now and then, we hear revived the standing controversy respecting the comparative merits of classics and mathematics. This controversy, however, is carried on in an empirical manner, with no reference to an ascertained criterion; and the question at issue is insignificant when compared with the general question of which it is part. To suppose that deciding whether a mathematical or a classical education is the best, is deciding what is the proper *curriculum*, is much the same thing as to suppose that the whole of dietetics lies in ascertaining whether or not bread is more nutritive than potatoes!

The question which we contend is of such transcendent moment, is, not whether such or such knowledge is of worth, but what is its *relative* worth? When they have named certain advantages which a given course of study has secured them, persons are apt to assume that they have justified themselves: quite forgetting that the adequateness of the advantages is the point to be judged. There is, perhaps, not a subject to which men devote attention that has not *some* value. A year diligently spent in getting up heraldry, would very possibly give a little further insight into ancient manners and morals. Any one who should learn the distances between all the towns in England, might, in the course of his life, find one or two of the thousand facts he had acquired of some slight service when arranging a journey. Gathering together all the small gossip of a county, profitless occupation as it would be, might yet occasionally help to establish some useful fact—say, a good example of hereditary transmission. But in these cases, every one would admit that there was no proportion between the required labour and the probable benefit. No one would tolerate the proposal to devote some years of a boy's time to getting such information, at the cost of much more valuable information which he might else have got. And if here the test of relative value is appealed to and held conclusive, then should it be appealed to and held conclusive throughout. Had we time to master all subjects we need not be particular.

In education, then, this is the question of questions, which it is high time we discussed in some methodic way. The first in importance, though the last to be considered, is the problem—how to decide among the conflicting claims of various subjects on our attention. Before there can be a rational *curriculum*, we must settle which things it most concerns us to know; or, to use a word of Bacon's, now unfortunately obsolete—we must determine the relative values of knowledges.

To this end, a measure of value is the first requisite. And happily, respecting the true measure of value, as expressed in general terms, there can be no dispute. Every one in contending for the worth of any particular order of information, does so by showing its bearing upon some part of life.

How to live?—that is the essential question for us. Not how to live in the mere material sense only, but in the widest sense. The general problem which comprehends every special problem is—the right ruling of conduct in all directions under all circumstances. In what way to treat the body; in what way to treat the mind; in what way to manage our affairs; in what way to bring up a family; in what way to behave as a citizen; in what way to utilise those sources of happiness which nature supplies —how to use all our faculties to the greatest advantage of ourselves and others—how to live completely? And this being the great thing needful for us to learn, is, by consequence, the great thing which education has to teach. To prepare us for complete living is the function which education has to discharge; and the only rational mode of judging of an educational course is, to judge in what degree it discharges such function.

This test, never used in its entirety, but rarely even partially used, and used then in a vague, half conscious way, has to be applied consciously, methodically, and throughout all cases. It behoves us to set before ourselves, and ever to keep clearly in view, complete living as the end to be achieved; so that in bringing up our children we may choose subjects and methods of instruction, with deliberate reference to this end. Not only ought we to cease from the mere unthinking adoption of the current fashion in education, which has no better warrant than any other fashion; but we must also rise above that rude, empirical style of judging displayed by those more intelligent people who do bestow some care in overseeing the cultivation of their children's minds. It must not suffice simply to *think* that such or such information will be useful in after life, or that this kind of knowledge is of more practical value than that; but we must seek out some process of estimating their respective values, so that as far as possible we may positively *know* which are most deserving of attention.

Our first step must obviously be to classify, in the order of their importance, the leading kinds of activity which constitute human life. They may be naturally arranged into:—1. those activities which directly minister to self-preservation; 2. those activities which, by securing the necessaries of life, indirectly minister to self-preservation; 3. those activities which have for their end the rearing and discipline of offspring; 4. those activities which are involved in the maintenance of proper social and political relations; 5. those miscellaneous activities which fill up the leisure part of life, devoted to the gratification of the tastes and feelings.

That these stand in something like their true order of subordination, it needs no long consideration to show. The actions and precautions by which, from moment to moment, we secure personal safety, must clearly take precedence of all others. Could there be a man, ignorant as an infant of surrounding objects and movements, or how to guide himself among them, he would pretty certainly lose his life the first time he went into the street; notwithstanding any amount of learning he might have on other matters. And as entire ignorance in all other directions would be less promptly fatal than entire ignorance in this direction, it must be admitted that knowledge immediately conducive to self-preservation is of primary importance.

That next after direct self-preservation comes the indirect self-preservation which consists in acquiring the means of living, none will question. That a man's industrial functions must be considered before his parental ones, is manifest from the fact that, speaking generally, the discharge of the parental functions is made possible only by the previous discharge of the industrial ones. The power of self-maintenance necessarily preceding the power of maintaining offspring, it follows that knowledge needful for self-maintenance has stronger claims than knowledge needful for family welfare—is second in value to none save knowledge needful for immediate self-preservation.

As the family comes before the State in order of time —as the bringing up of children is possible before the State exists, or when it has ceased to be, whereas the State is rendered possible only by the bringing up of children; it follows that the duties of the parent demand closer attention than those of the citizen. Or, to use a further argument—since the goodness of a society ultimately depends on the nature of its citizens; and since the nature of its citizens is more modifiable by early training than by anything else; we must conclude that the welfare of the family underlies the welfare of society. And hence knowledge directly conducing to the first, must take precedence of knowledge directly conducing to the last.

Those various forms of pleasurable occupation which fill up the leisure left by graver occupations—the enjoyments of music, poetry, painting, etc.—manifestly imply a pre-existing society. Not only is a considerable development of them impossible without a long-established social union; but their very subject-matter consists in great part of social sentiments and sympathies. Not only does society supply the conditions to their growth; but also the ideas and sentiments they express. And, consequently, that part of human conduct which constitutes good citizenship, is of more moment than that which goes out in accomplishments or exercise of the tastes; and, in education, preparation for the one must rank before preparation for the other.

We do not mean to say that these divisions are definitely separable. We do not deny that they are intricately entangled with each other, in such way that there can be no training for any that is not in some measure a training for all. Nor do we question that of each division there are portions more important than certain portions of the preceding divisions: that, for instance, a man of much skill in business but little other faculty, may fall further below the standard of complete living than one of but moderate ability in money-getting but great judgment as a parent; or that exhaustive information bearing on right social action, joined with entire want of general culture in literature and the fine arts, is less desirable than a more moderate share of the one joined with some of the other. But, after making due qualifications, there still remain these broadly-marked divisions; and it still continues substantially true that these divisions subordinate one another in the foregoing order, because the corresponding divisions of life make one another *possible* in that order.

Of course the ideal of education is—complete preparation in all these divisions. But failing this ideal, as in our phase of civilisation every one must do more or less, the aim should be to maintain *a due proportion* between the degrees of preparation in each. Not exhaustive cultivation in any one, supremely important though it may be—not even an exclusive attention to the two, three, or four divisions of greatest importance; but an attention to all:—greatest where the value is greatest; less where the value is less; least where the value is least. For the average man (not to forget the cases in which peculiar aptitude for some one department of knowledge, rightly makes pursuit of that one the bread-winning occupation) —for the average man, we say, the desideratum is, a training that approaches nearest to perfection in the things which most subserve complete living, and falls more and more below perfection in the things that have more and more remote bearings on complete living.

In regulating education by this standard, there are some general considerations that should be ever present to us. The worth of any kind of culture, as aiding complete living, may be either necessary or more or less contingent. There is knowledge of intrinsic value; knowledge of quasi-intrinsic value; and knowledge of conventional value. Such facts as that sensations of numbness and tingling commonly precede paralysis, that the resistance of water to a body moving through it varies as the square of the velocity, that chlorine is a disinfectant,—these, and the truths of Science in general, are of intrinsic value: they will bear on human conduct ten thousand years hence as they do now. The extra knowledge of our own language, which is given by an acquaintance with

Latin and Greek, may be considered to have a value that is quasi-intrinsic: it must exist for us and for other races whose languages owe much to these sources; but will last only as long as our languages last. While that kind of information which, in our schools, usurps the name History —the mere tissue of names and dates and dead unmeaning events—has a conventional value only: it has not the remotest bearing on any of our actions; and is of use only for the avoidance of those unpleasant criticisms which current opinion passes upon its absence. Of course, as those facts which concern all mankind throughout all time must be held of greater moment than those which concern only a portion of them during a limited era, and of far greater moment than those which concern only a portion of them during the continuance of a fashion; it follows that in a rational estimate, knowledge of intrinsic worth must, other things equal, take precedence of knowledge that is of quasi-intrinsic or conventional worth.

One further preliminary. Acquirement of every kind has two values—value as *knowledge* and value as *discipline*. Besides its use for guiding conduct, the acquisition of each order of facts has also its use as mental exercise; and its effects as a preparative for complete living have to be considered under both these heads.

These, then, are the general ideas with which we must set out in discussing a *curriculum:*—Life as divided into several kinds of activity of successively decreasing importance; the worth of each order of facts as regulating these several kinds of activity, intrinsically, quasi-intrinsically, and conventionally; and their regulative influences estimated both as knowledge and discipline.

Happily, that all-important part of education which goes to secure direct self-preservation, is in great part already provided for. Too momentous to be left to our blundering, Nature takes it into her own hands.

This, however, is by no means all that is comprehended in the education that prepares for direct self-preservation. Besides guarding the body against mechanical damage or destruction, it has to be guarded against injury from other causes—against the disease and death that follow breaches of physiologic law. For complete living it is necessary, not only that sudden annihilations of life shall be warded off; but also that there shall be escaped the incapacities and the slow annihilation which unwise habits entail. As, without health and energy, the industrial, the parental, the social, and all other activities become more or less impossible; it is clear that this secondary kind of direct self-preservation is only less important than the primary kind; and that knowledge tending to secure it should rank very high.

If any one doubts the importance of an acquaintance with the principles of physiology, as a means to complete living, let him look around and see how many men and women he can find in middle or later life who are thoroughly well. Only occasionally do we meet with an example of vigorous health continued to old age; hourly do we meet with examples of acute disorder, chronic ailment, general debility, premature decrepitude. Scarcely is there one to whom you put the question, who has not, in the course of his life, brought upon himself illnesses which a little information would have saved him from.

Hence, knowledge which subserves direct self-preservation by preventing this loss of health, is of primary importance. We do not contend that possession of such knowledge would by any means wholly remedy the evil. It is clear that in our present phase of civilisation, men's necessities often compel them to transgress. And it is further clear that, even in the absence of such compulsion, their inclinations would frequently lead them, spite of their convictions, to sacrifice future good to present gratification. But we *do* contend that the right knowledge impressed in the right way would effect much; and we further contend that as the laws of health must be recognised before they can be fully conformed to, the imparting of such knowledge must precede a more rational living—come when that may. We infer that as vigorous health and its accompanying high spirits are larger elements of happiness than any other things whatever, the teaching how to maintain them is a teaching that yields in moment to no other whatever. And therefore we assert that such a course of physiology as is needful for the comprehension of its general truths, and their bearings on daily conduct, is an all-essential part of a rational education.

Strange that the assertion should need making! Stranger still that it should need defending! Yet are there not a few by whom such a proposition will be received with something approaching to derision. Men who would blush if caught saying Iphigénia instead of Iphigenía, or would resent as an insult any imputation of ignorance respecting the fabled labours of a fabled demigod, show not the slightest shame in confessing that they do not know where the Eustachian tubes are, what are the actions of the spinal cord, what is the normal rate of pulsation, or how the lungs are inflated. While anxious that their sons should be well up in the superstitions of two thousand years ago, they care not that they should be taught anything about the structure and functions of their own bodies—nay, even wish them not to be so taught. So overwhelming is the influence of established routine! So terribly in our education does the ornamental over-ride the useful!

We need not insist on the value of that knowledge which aids indirect self-preservation by facilitating the gaining of a livelihood. This is admitted by all; and, indeed, by the mass is perhaps too exclusively regarded as the end of education. But while every one is ready to endorse the abstract proposition that instruction fitting youths for the business of life is of high importance, or even to consider it of supreme importance; yet scarcely any inquire what instruction will so fit them. It is true that reading, writing, and arithmetic are taught with an intelligent appreciation of their uses. But when we have said this we have said nearly all. While the great bulk of what else is acquired has no bearing on the industrial activities, an immensity of information that has a direct bearing on the industrial activities is entirely passed over.

For, leaving out only some very small classes, what are all men employed in? They are employed in the production, preparation, and distribution of commodities. And on what does efficiency in the production, preparation, and distribution of commodities depend? It depends on the use of methods fitted to the respective natures of these commodities; it depends on an adequate acquaintance with their physical, chemical, or vital properties, as the case may be; that is, it depends on Science. This order of knowledge which is in great part ignored in our school-courses, is the order of knowledge underlying the right performance of those processes by which civilised life is made possible.

Passing over the most abstract science, Logic, on the due guidance by which, however, the large producer or distributor depends, knowingly or unknowingly, for success in his business-forecasts, we come first to Mathematics. Of this, the most general division, dealing with number, guides all industrial activities; be they those by which processes are adjusted, or estimates framed, or commodities bought and sold, or accounts kept.

For the higher arts of construction, some acquaintance with the more special division of Mathematics is indispensable. The village carpenter, who lays out his work by empirical rules, equally with the builder of a Britannia Bridge, makes hourly reference to the laws of space-relations. The surveyor who measures the land purchased; the architect in designing a mansion to be built on it; the builder when laying out the foundations; the masons in cutting the stones; and the various artizans who put up the fittings; are all guided by geometrical truths.

Turn next to the Abstract-Concrete sciences. On the application of the simplest of these, Mechanics, depends the success of modern manufactures. The properties of the lever, the wheel-and-axle, etc., are recognised in every machine, and to machinery in these times we owe all production. Trace the history of the breakfast-roll. The soil out of which it came was drained with machine-made tiles; the surface was turned over by a machine; the wheat was reaped, thrashed, and winnowed by machines; by machinery it was ground and bolted; and had the flour been sent to Gosport, it might have been made into biscuits by a machine. Look round the room in which you sit. If modern, probably the bricks in its walls were machine-made; and by machinery the flooring was sawn and planed, the mantel-shelf sawn and polished, the paper-hangings made and printed. The veneer on the table, the turned legs of the chairs, the carpet, the curtains, are all products of machinery. Your clothing—plain, figured, or printed—is it not wholly woven, nay, perhaps even sewed, by machinery? And the volume you are reading—are not its leaves fabricated by one machine and covered with these words by another? Add to which that for the means of distribution over both land and sea, we are similarly indebted. And then observe that according as knowledge of mechanics is well or ill applied to these ends, comes success or failure. The engineer who miscalculates the strength of materials, builds a bridge that breaks down. The manufacturer who uses a bad machine cannot compete with another whose machine wastes less in friction and inertia. The ship-builder adhering to the old model is out-sailed by one who builds on the mechanically-justified wave-line principle. And as the ability of a nation to hold its own against other nations, depends on the skilled activity of its units, we see that on mechanical knowledge may turn the national fate.

On ascending from the divisions of Abstract-Concrete science dealing with molar forces, to those divisions of it which deal with molecular forces, we come to another vast series of applications. To this group of sciences joined with the preceding groups we owe the steam-engine, which does the work of millions of labourers. That section of physics which formulates the laws of heat, has taught us how to economise fuel in various industries; how to increase the produce of smelting furnaces by substituting the hot for the cold blast; how to ventilate mines; how to prevent explosions by using the safety-lamp; and, through the thermometer, how to regulate innumerable processes. That section which has the phenomena of light for its subject, gives eyes to the old and the myopic; aids through the microscope in detecting diseases and adulterations; and, by improved lighthouses, prevents shipwrecks. Researches in electricity and magnetism have saved innumerable lives and incalculable property through the compass; have subserved many arts by the electrotype; and now, in the telegraph, have supplied us with an agency by which for the future, mercantile transactions will be regulated and political intercourse carried on. While in the details of in-door life, from the improved kitchen-range up to the stereoscope on the drawing-room table, the applications of advanced physics underlie our comforts and gratifications.

Still more numerous are the applications of Chemistry. Indeed, there is now scarcely any manufacture over some part of which chemistry does not preside. Nay, in these times even agriculture, to be profitably carried on, must have like guidance.

Of the Concrete sciences, we come first to Astronomy. Out of this has grown that art of navigation which has made possible the enormous foreign commerce that supports a large part of our population, while supplying us with many necessaries and most of our luxuries.

Geology, again, is a science knowledge of which greatly aids industrial success. . . .

And then the science of life—Biology: does not this, too, bear fundamentally on these processes of indirect self-preservation? With what we ordinarily call manufactures, it has, indeed, little connection; but with the all-essential manufacture—that of food—it is inseparably connected. As agriculture must conform its methods to the phenomena of vegetal and animal life, it follows that the science of these phenomena is the rational basis of agriculture.

Yet one more science have we to note as bearing directly on industrial success—the Science of Society. Men who daily look at the state of the money-market; glance over prices current; discuss the probable crops of corn, cotton, sugar, wool, silk; weigh the chances of war; and from these data decide on their mercantile operations; are students of social science: . . .

Thus, to all such as are occupied in the production, exchange, or distribution of commodities, acquaintance with Science in some of it departments, is of fundamental importance. Each man who is immediately or remotely implicated in any form of industry (and few are not) has in some way to deal with the mathematical, physical, and chemical properties of things; perhaps, also, has a direct interest in biology; and certainly has in sociology. Whether he does or does not succeed well in that indirect self-preservation which we call getting a good livelihood, depends in a great degree on his knowledge of one or more of these sciences: not, it may be, a rational knowledge; but still a knowledge, though empirical. For what we call learning a business, really implies learning the science involved in it; though not perhaps under the name of science. And hence a grounding in science is of great importance, both because it prepares for all this, and because rational knowledge has an immense superiority over empirical knowledge. Moreover, not only is scientific culture requisite for each, that he may understand the *how* and the *why* of the things and processes with which he is concerned as maker or distributor; but it is often of much moment that he should understand the *how* and the *why* of various other things and processes. In this age of joint-stock undertakings, nearly every man above the labourer is interested as capitalist in some other occupation than his own; and, as thus interested, his profit or loss often depends on his knowledge of the sciences bearing on this other occupation.

That which our school-courses leave almost entirely out, we thus find to be that which most nearly concerns the business of life. Our industries would cease, were it not for the information which men begin to acquire, as they best may, after their education is said to be finished. And were it not for this information, from age to age accumulated and spread by unofficial means, these industries would never have existed. Had there been no teaching but such as goes on in our public schools, England would now be what it was in feudal times. That increasing acquaintance with the laws of phenomena, which has through successive ages enabled us to subjugate Nature to our needs, and in these days gives the common labourer comforts which a few centuries ago kings could not purchase, is scarcely in any degree owed to the appointed means of instructing our youth. The vital knowledge—that by which we have grown as a nation to what we are, and which now underlies our whole existence, is a knowledge that has got itself taught in nooks and corners; while the ordained agencies for teaching have been mumbling little else but dead formulas.

We come now to the third great division of human activities—a division for which no preparation whatever is made. If by some strange chance not a vestige of us descended to the remote future save a pile of our schoolbooks or some college examination papers, we may imagine how puzzled an antiquary of the period would be on finding in them no sign that the learners were ever likely to be parents. "This must have been the *curriculum* for their celibates," we may fancy him concluding. "I perceive here an elaborate preparation for many things; especially for reading the books of extinct nations and of co-existing nations (from which indeed it seems clear that these people had very little worth reading in their own tongue); but I find no reference whatever to the bringing up of children. They could not have been so absurd as to omit all training for this gravest of responsibilities. Evidently then, this was the school-course of one of their monastic orders."

Equally great are the ignorance and the consequent injury, when we turn from physical training to moral training. Consider the young mother and her nursery-legislation. But a few years ago she was at school, where her memory was crammed with words, and names, and dates, and her reflective faculties scarcely in the slightest degree exercised—where not one idea was given her respecting the methods of dealing with the opening mind of childhood; and where her discipline did not in the least fit her for thinking out methods of her own. The intervening years have been passed in practising music, in fancy-work, in novel-reading, and in party-going: no thought having yet been given to the grave responsibilities of maternity; and scarcely any of that solid intellectual culture obtained which would be some preparation for such responsibilities. And now see her with an unfolding human character committed to her charge—see her profoundly ignorant of the phenomena with which she has to deal, undertaking to do that which can be done but imperfectly even with the aid of the profoundest knowledge. She knows nothing about the nature of the emotions, their order of evolution, their functions, or where use ends and abuse begins. She is under the impression that some of the feelings are wholly bad, which is not true of any one of them; and that others are good however far they may be carried, which is also not true of any one of them. And then, ignorant as she is of the structure she has to deal with, she is equally ignorant of the effects produced on it by this or that treatment. What can be more inevitable than the disastrous results we see hourly arising? Lacking knowledge of mental phenomena, with their cause and consequences, her interference is frequently more mischievous than absolute passivity would have been. This and that kind of action, which are quite normal and beneficial, she perpetually thwarts; and so diminishes the child's happiness and profit,

injures its temper and her own, and produces estrange-
ment. Deeds which she thinks it desirable to encourage,
she gets performed by threats and bribes, or by exciting a
desire for applause: considering little what the inward
motive may be, so long as the outward conduct conforms; and thus cultivating hypocrisy, and fear, and
selfishness, in place of good feeling. While insisting on
truthfulness, she constantly sets an example of untruth by
threatening penalties which she does not inflict. While
inculcating self-control, she hourly visits on her little ones
angry scoldings for acts undeserving of them. She has
not the remotest idea that in the nursery, as in the world,
that alone is the truly salutary discipline which visits on
all conduct, good and bad, the natural consequences
—the consequences, pleasurable or painful, which in the
nature of things such conduct tends to bring. Being thus
without theoretic guidance, and quite incapable of guiding herself by tracing the mental processes going on in
her children, her rule is impulsive, inconsistent, mischievous; and would indeed be generally ruinous were it
not that the overwhelming tendency of the growing
mind to assume the moral type of the race usually sub-
ordinates all minor influences.

And then the culture of the intellect—is not this, too,
mismanaged in a similar manner? Grant that the phenomena of intelligence conform to laws; grant that the
evolution of intelligence in a child also conforms to laws;
and it follows inevitably that education cannot be rightly
guided without a knowledge of these laws. To suppose
that you can properly regulate this process of forming
and accumulating ideas, without understanding the nature
of the process, is absurd. How widely, then, must teaching as it is differ from teaching as it should be; when
hardly any parents, and but few tutors, know anything

about psychology. As might be expected, the established system is grievously at fault, alike in matter and in manner. While the right class of facts is withheld, the wrong class is forcibly administered in the wrong way and in the wrong order. Under that common limited idea of education which confines it to knowledge gained from books, parents thrust primers into the hands of their little ones years too soon, to their great injury. Not recognizing the truth that the function of books is supplementary—that they form an indirect means to knowledge when direct means fail—a means of seeing through other men what you cannot see for yourself; teachers are eager to give second-hand facts in place of first-hand facts. Not perceiving the enormous value of that spontaneous education which goes on in early years—not perceiving that a child's restless observation, instead of being ignored or checked, should be diligently ministered to, and made as accurate and complete as possible; they insist on occupying its eyes and thoughts with things that are, for the time being, incomprehensible and repugnant. Possessed by a superstition which worships the symbols of knowledge instead of the knowledge itself, they do not see that only when his acquaintance with the objects and processes of the household, the streets, and the fields, is becoming tolerably exhaustive—only then should a child be introduced to the new sources of information which books supply: and this, not only because immediate cognition is of far greater value than mediate cognition; but also, because the words contained in books can be rightly interpreted into ideas, only in proportion to the antecedent experience of things. Observe next, that this formal instruction, far too soon commenced, is carried on with but little reference to the laws of mental development. Intellectual progress is of necessity from the concrete to the abstract. But regardless of this, highly abstract studies, such as grammar, which should come quite late, are begun quite early. Political geography, dead and uninteresting to a child, and which should be an appendage of sociological studies, is commenced betimes; while physical geography, comprehensible and comparatively attractive to a child, is in great part passed over. Nearly every subject dealt with is arranged in abnormal order: definitions and rules and principles being put first, instead of being disclosed, as they are in the order of nature, through the study of cases. And then, pervading the whole, is the vicious system of rote learning—a system of sacrificing the spirit to the letter. See the results. What with perceptions unnaturally dulled by early thwarting, and a coerced attention to books—what with the mental confusion produced by teaching subjects before they can be understood, and in each of them giving generalisations before the facts of which they are the generalisations—what with making the pupil a mere passive recipient of other's ideas, and not in the least leading him to be an active inquirer or self-instructor—and what with taxing the faculties to excess; there are very few minds that become as efficient as they might be. Examinations being once passed, books are laid aside; the greater part of what has been acquired, being unorganised, soon drops out of recollection; what remains is mostly inert—the art of applying knowledge not having been cultivated; and there is but little power either of accurate observation or independent thinking. To all which add, that while much of the information gained is of relatively small value, an immense mass of information of transcendent value is entirely passed over.

Thus we find the facts to be such as might have been inferred *à priori*. The training of children—physical, moral, and intellectual—is dreadfully defective. And in great measure it is so because parents are devoid of that knowledge by which this training can alone be rightly guided.

From the parental functions let us pass now to the functions of the citizen. We have here to inquire what knowledge fits a man for the discharge of these functions. It cannot be alleged that the need for knowledge fitting him for these functions is wholly overlooked; for our school-courses contain certain studies, which, nominally at least, bear upon political and social duties. Of these the only one that occupies a prominent place is History.

But, as already hinted, the information commonly given under this head, is almost valueless for purposes of guidance. Scarcely any of the facts set down in our school-histories, and very few of those contained in the more elaborate works written for adults, illustrate the right principles of political action. The biographies of monarchs (and our children learn little else) throw scarcely any light upon the science of society. Familiarity with court intrigues, plots, usurpations, or the like, and with all the personalities accompanying them, aids very little in elucidating the causes of national progress. If not, then it must be admitted that the liking felt for certain classes of historical facts is no proof of their worth; and that we must test their worth, as we test the worth of other facts, by asking to what uses they are applicable. Were some one to tell you that your neighbour's cat kittened yesterday, you would say the information was valueless. Fact though it might be, you would call it an utterly useless fact—a fact that could in no way influence your actions in life—a fact that would not help you in learning how to live completely. Well, apply the same

test to the great mass of historical facts, and you will get
the same result. They are facts from which no conclusions
can be drawn—*unorganisable* facts; and therefore facts
of no service in establishing principles of conduct, which
is the chief use of facts. Read them, if you like, for amuse-
ment; but do not flatter yourself they are instructive.

That which constitutes History, properly so called, is
in great part omitted from works on the subject. Only of
late years have historians commenced giving us, in any
considerable quantity, the truly valuable information.
As in past ages the king was everything and the people
nothing; so, in past histories the doings of the king fill
the entire picture, to which the national life forms but
an obscure background. While only now, when the welfare of nations rather than of rulers is becoming the
dominant idea, are historians beginning to occupy themselves with the phenomena of social progress. The thing
it really concerns us to know is the natural history of
society. We want all facts which help us to understand
how a nation has grown and organised itself. Among
these, let us of course have an account of its government;
with as little as may be of gossip about the men who
officered it, and as much as possible about the structure,
principles, methods, prejudices, corruptions, etc., which
it exhibited: and let this account include not only the
nature and actions of the central government, but also
those of local governments, down to their minutest ramifications. Let us of course also have a parallel description
of the ecclesiastical government—its organisation, its conduct, its power, its relations to the State; and accompanying this, the ceremonial, creed, and religious ideas—not
only those nominally believed, but those really believed
and acted upon. Let us at the same time be informed of
the control exercised by class over class, as displayed in

social observances—in titles, salutations, and forms of address. Let us know, too, what were all the other customs which regulated the popular life out of doors and in-doors: including those concerning the relations of the sexes, and the relations of parents to children. The superstitions, also, from the more important myths down to the charms in common use, should be indicated. Next should come a delineation of the industrial system: showing to what extent the division of labour was carried; how trades were regulated, whether by caste, guilds, or otherwise; what was the connection between employers and employed; what were the agencies for distributing commodities; what were the means of communication; what was the circulating medium. Accompanying all which should be given an account of the industrial arts technically considered: stating the processes in use, and the quality of the products. Further, the intellectual condition of the nation in its various grades should be depicted; not only with respect to the kind and amount of education, but with respect to the progress made in science, and the prevailing manner of thinking. The degree of æsthetic culture, as displayed in architecture, sculpture, painting, dress, music, poetry, and fiction, should be described. Nor should there be omitted a sketch of the daily lives of the people—their food, their homes, and their amusements. And lastly, to connect the whole, should be exhibited the morals, theoretical and practical, of all classes: as indicated in their laws, habits, proverbs, deeds. These facts, given with as much brevity as consists with clearness and accuracy, should be so grouped and arranged that they may be comprehended in their *ensemble,* and contemplated as mutually-dependent parts of one great whole. The aim should be so to present them that men may readily trace the *consensus* subsisting

among them; with the view of learning what social phenomena co-exist with what other. And then the corresponding delineations of succeeding ages should be so
managed as to show how each belief, institution, custom,
and arrangement was modified; and how the *consensus*
of preceding structures and functions was developed into
the *consensus* of succeeding ones. Such alone is the kind
of information respecting past times which can be of
service to the citizen for the regulation of his conduct.
The only history that is of practical value is what may be
called Descriptive Sociology. And the highest office
which the historian can discharge, is that of so nar-
rating the lives of nations, as to furnish materials for a
Comparative Sociology; and for the subsequent determination of the ultimate laws to which social phenomena
conform.

But now mark, that even supposing an adequate stock
of this truly valuable historical knowledge has been acquired, it is of comparatively little use without the key.
And the key is to be found only in Science. In the absence
of the generalisations of biology and psychology, rational
interpretation of social phenomena is impossible. Only
in proportion as men draw certain rude, empirical inferences respecting human nature, are they enabled to
understand even the simplest facts of social life: as, for
instance, the relation between supply and demand. And
if the most elementary truths of sociology cannot be
reached until some knowledge is obtained of how men
generally think, feel, and act under given circumstances;
then it is manifest that there can be nothing like a wide
comprehension of sociology, unless through a competent
acquaintance with man in all his faculties, bodily, and
mental. Consider the matter in the abstract, and this conclusion is self-evident. Thus:—Society is made up of in-

dividuals; all that is done in society is done by the combined actions of individuals; and therefore, in individual actions only can be found the solutions of social phenomena. But the actions of individuals depend on the laws of their natures; and their actions cannot be understood until these laws are understood. These laws, however, when reduced to their simplest expressions, prove to be corollaries from the laws of body and mind in general. Hence it follows that biology and psychology are indispensable as interpreters of sociology. Or, to state the conclusions still more simply:—all social phenomena are phenomena of life—are the most complex manifestations of life—must conform to the laws of life—and can be understood only when the laws of life are understood. Thus, then, for the regulation of this fourth division of human activities, we are, as before, dependent on Science.

And now we come to that remaining division of human life which includes the relaxations and amusements filling leisure hours. After considering what training best fits for self-preservation, for the obtainment of sustenance, for the discharge of parental duties, and for the regulation of social and political conduct; we have now to consider what training best fits for the miscellaneous ends not included in these—for the enjoyment of Nature, of Literature, and of the Fine Arts, in all their forms. Postponing them as we do to things that bear more vitally upon human welfare; and bringing everything, as we have, to the test of actual value; it will perhaps be inferred that we are inclined to slight these less essential things. No greater mistake could be made, however. We yield to none in the value we attach to æsthetic culture and its pleasures. Without painting, sculpture, music, poetry, and the emotions produced by natural beauty of every kind, life would lose half its charm. So far from

regarding the training and gratification of the tastes as
unimportant, we believe that in time to come they will
occupy a much larger share of human life than now.
When the forces of Nature have been fully conquered
to man's use—when the means of production have been
brought to perfection—when labour has been econo-
mised to the highest degree—when education has been so
systematised that a preparation for the more essential
activities may be made with comparative rapidity—and
when, consequently, there is a great increase of spare
time; then will the beautiful, both in Art and Nature,
rightly fill a large space in the minds of all.

But it is one thing to approve of æsthetic culture as
largely conducive to human happiness; and another
thing to admit that it is a fundamental requisite to
human happiness. However important it may be, it must
yield precedence to those kinds of culture which bear
directly upon daily duties. As before hinted, literature
and the fine arts are made possible by those activities
which make individual and social life possible; and manifestly, that which is made possible, must be postponed
to that which makes it possible. Architecture, sculpture,
painting, music, and poetry, may truly be called the
efflorescence of civilised life. But even supposing they
are of such transcendent worth as to subordinate the
civilised life out of which they grow (which can hardly
be asserted), it will still be admitted that the production
of a healthy civilised life must be the first consideration;
and that culture subserving this must occupy the highest
place.

And here we see most distinctly the vice of our educational system. It neglects the plant for the sake of the
flower. In anxiety for elegance, it forgets substance.
While it gives no knowledge conducive to self-preserva-

tion—while of knowledge that facilitates gaining a liveli-hood it gives but the rudiments, and leaves the greater part to be picked up any how in after life—while for the discharge of parental functions it makes not the slightest provision—and while for the duties of citizenship it pre-pares by imparting a mass of facts, most of which are irrele-vant, and the rest without a key; it is diligent in teach-ing whatever adds to refinement, polish, éclat. Fully as we may admit that extensive acquaintance with modern languages is a valuable accomplishment, which, through reading, conversation, and travel, aids in giving a certain finish; it by no means follows that this result is rightly purchased at the cost of the vitally important knowledge sacrificed to it. Supposing it true that classical education conduces to elegance and correctness of style; it cannot be said that elegance and correctness of style are com-parable in importance to a familiarity with the prin-ciples that should guide the rearing of children. Grant that the taste may be improved by reading the poetry written in extinct languages; yet it is not to be inferred that such improvement of taste is equivalent in value to an acquaintance with the laws of health. Accomplish-ments, the fine arts, *belles-lettres,* and all those things which, as we say, constitute the efflorescence of civilisa-tion, should be wholly subordinate to that instruction and discipline in which civilisation rests. *As they occupy the leisure part of life, so should they occupy the leisure part of education.*

Recognising thus the true position of æsthetics, and holding that while the cultivation of them should form a part of education from its commencement, such cultiva-tion should be subsidiary; we have now to inquire what knowledge is of most use to this end—what knowledge best fits for this remaining sphere of activity? To this

question the answer is still the same as heretofore. Un-
expected though the assertion may be, it is nevertheless
true, that the highest Art of every kind is based on Science
—that without Science there can be neither perfect production nor full appreciation. Science, in that limited
acceptation current in society, may not have been possessed by various artists of high repute; but acute observers
as such artists have been, they have always possessed a
stock of those empirical generalisations which constitute science in its lowest phase; and they have habitually
fallen far below perfection, partly because their generalisations were comparatively few and inaccurate. That
science necessarily underlies the fine arts, becomes manifest, *à priori,* when we remember that art-products are
all more or less representative of objective or subjective
phenomena; that they can be good only in proportion as
they conform to the laws of these phenomena; and that
before they can thus conform, the artist must know what
these laws are.

Youths preparing for the practice of sculpture have to
acquaint themselves with the bones and muscles of the
human frame in their distribution, attachments, and
movements. This is a portion of science; and it has been
found needful to impart it for the prevention of those
many errors which sculptors who do not possess it commit. A knowledge of mechanical principles is also requisite; and such knowledge not being usually possessed,
grave mechanical mistakes are frequently made.

In painting, the necessity for scientific information, empirical if not rational, is still more conspicuous. What
gives the grotesqueness of Chinese pictures, unless their
utter disregard of the laws of appearances—their absurd linear perspective, and their want of aerial perspective? In what are the drawings of a child so faulty, if not

in a similar absence of truth—an absence arising, in great part, from ignorance of the way in which the aspects of things vary with the conditions? Do but remember the books and lectures by which students are instructed; or consider the criticisms of Ruskin; or look at the doings of the Pre-Raffaelites; and you will see that progress in painting implies increasing knowledge of how effects in Nature are produced.

To say that music, too, has need of scientific aid will cause still more surprise. Yet it may be shown that music is but an idealisation of the natural language of emotion; and that consequently, music must be good or bad according as it conforms to the laws of this natural language. They sin against science by setting to music ideas that are not emotional enough to prompt musical expression; and they also sin against science by using musical phrases that have no natural relations to the ideas expressed: even where these are emotional. They are bad because they are untrue. And to say they are untrue, is to say they are unscientific.

Even in poetry the same thing holds. Like music, poetry has its roots in those natural modes of expression which accompany deep feeling. Its rhythm, its strong and numerous metaphors, its hyperboles, its violent inversions, are simply exaggerations of the traits of excited speech. To be good, therefore, poetry must pay attention to those laws of nervous action which excited speech obeys.

Not only is it that the artist, of whatever kind, cannot produce a truthful work without he understands the laws of the phenomena he represents; but it is that he must also understand how the minds of spectators or listeners will be affected by the several peculiarities of his work—a question in psychology. What impression any art-product generates, manifestly depends upon the mental natures of those to whom it is presented; and as all mental natures have certain characteristics in common, there must result certain corresponding general principles on which alone art-products can be successfully framed. These general principles cannot be fully understood and applied, unless the artist sees how they follow from the laws of mind.

We do not for a moment believe that science will make an artist. While we contend that the leading laws both of objective and subjective phenomena must be understood by him, we by no means contend that knowledge of such laws will serve in place of natural perception. Not the poet only, but the artist of every type, is born, not made. What we assert is, that innate faculty cannot dispense with the aid of organised knowledge. Intuition will do much, but it will not do all. Only when Genius is married to Science can the highest results be produced.

And now let us not overlook the further great fact, that not only does science underlie sculpture, painting, music, poetry, but that science is itself poetic. The current opinion that science and poetry are opposed, is a delusion. It is doubtless true that as states of consciousness, cognition and emotion tend to exclude each other. And it is doubtless also true that an extreme activity of the reflective powers tends to deaden the feelings; while an extreme activity of the feelings tends to deaden the reflective powers: in which sense, indeed, all orders of activity are antagonistic to each other. But it is not true that the facts of science are unpoetical; or that the cultivation of science is necessarily unfriendly to the exercise of imagination and the love of the beautiful. On the contrary, science opens up realms of poetry where to the unscientific all is a blank. Those engaged in scientific researches constantly show us that they realise not less vividly, but more vividly, than others, the poetry of their subjects. Whoso will dip into Hugh Miller's works of geology, or read Mr. Lewes's *Sea-side Studies,* will perceive that science excites poetry rather than extinguishes it. And he who contemplates the life of Goethe, must see that the poet and the man of science can co-exist in equal activity. Is it not, indeed, an absurd and almost a sacrilegious belief, that the more a man studies Nature the less he reveres it?

We find then, that even for this remaining division of human activities, scientific culture is the proper preparation. We find that æsthetics in general are necessarily based upon scientific principles; and can be pursued with complete success only through an acquaintance with these principles. We find that for the criticism and due appreciation of works of art, a knowledge of the constitution of things, or in other words, a knowledge of science, is requisite. And we not only find that science is the handmaid to all forms of art and poetry, but that, rightly regarded, science is itself poetic.

Thus far our question has been, the worth of knowledge of this or that kind for purposes of guidance. We have now to judge the relative value of different kinds of knowledge for purposes of discipline. This division of our subject we are obliged to treat with comparative brevity; and happily, no very lengthened treatment of it is needed. Having found what is best for the one end, we have by implication found what is best for the other. We may be quite sure that the acquirement of those classes of facts which are most useful for regulating conduct involves a mental exercise best fitted for strengthening the faculties. It would be utterly contrary to the beautiful economy of Nature, if one kind of culture were needed for the gaining of information and another kind were needed as a mental gymnastic. Everywhere throughout creation we find faculties developed through the performance of those functions which it is their office to perform; not through the performance of artificial exercises devised to fit them for those functions.

One advantage claimed for that devotion to language-learning which forms so prominent a feature in the ordinary *curriculum,* is, that the memory is thereby strengthened. This is assumed to be an advantage peculiar to the study of words. But the truth is, that the sciences afford far wider fields for the exercise of memory. It is no slight task to remember everything about our solar system; much more to remember all that is known concerning the structure of our galaxy. Each leading division of physics—sound, heat, light, electricity—includes facts numerous enough to alarm any one proposing to learn them all. And when we pass to the organic sciences, the effort of memory required becomes still greater. In human anatomy alone, the quantity of detail is so great, that the young surgeon has commonly to get it up half-a-dozen times before he can permanently retain it.

But now mark that while, for the training of mere memory, science is as good as, if not better than, language; it has an immense superiority in the kind of memory it trains. In the acquirement of a language, the connections of ideas to be established in the mind correspond to facts that are in great measure accidental; whereas, in the acquirement of science, the connections of ideas to be established in the mind correspond to facts that are mostly necessary. While language familiarises with non-rational relations, science familiarises with rational relations. While the one exercises memory only, the other exercises both memory and understanding.

Observe next, that a great superiority of science over language as a means of discipline, is, that it cultivates the judgment. As, in a lecture on mental education delivered at the Royal Institution, Professor Faraday well remarks, the most common intellectual fault is deficiency of judgment. "Society, speaking generally," he says, "is not only ignorant as respects education of the judgment, but it is also ignorant of its ignorance." And the cause to which he ascribes this state, is want of scientific culture. The truth of his conclusion is obvious. Correct judgment with regard to surrounding objects, events, and consequences, becomes possible only through knowledge of the way in which surrounding phenomena depend on each other. No extent of acquaintance with the meanings of words, will guarantee correct inferences respecting causes and effects. The habit of drawing conclusions from data, and then of verifying those conclusions by observation and experiment, can alone give the power of judging correctly. And that it necessitates this habit is one of the immense advantages of science.

Not only, however, for intellectual discipline is science the best; but also for *moral* discipline. The learning of languages tends, if anything, further to increase the already undue respect for authority. Such and such are the meanings of these words, says the teacher of the dictionary. So and so is the rule in this case, says the grammar. By the pupil these dicta are received as unquestionable. His constant attitude of mind is that of submission to dogmatic teaching. And a necessary result is a tendency to accept without inquiry whatever is established. Quite opposite is the mental tone generated by the cultivation of science. Science makes constant appeal to individual reason. Its truths are not accepted on authority alone; but all are at liberty to test them—nay, in many cases, the pupil is required to think out his own conclusions. Every step in a scientific investigation is submitted to his judgment. He is not asked to admit it without seeing it to be true. And the trust in his own powers thus produced is further increased by the uniformity with which Nature justifies his inferences when they are correctly drawn. From all which there flows that independence which is a most valuable element in character. Nor is this the only moral benefit bequeathed by scientific culture. When carried on, as it should always be, as much as possible under the form of original research, it exercises perseverance and sincerity.

Lastly we have to assert—and the assertion will, we doubt not, cause extreme surprise—that the discipline of science is superior to that of our ordinary education, because of the *religious* culture that it gives. Of course we do not here use the words scientific and religious in their ordinary limited acceptations; but in their widest and highest acceptations. Doubtless, to the superstitions that pass under the name of religion, science is antagonistic; but not to the essential religion which these superstitions merely hide. Doubtless, too, in much of the science that is current, there is a pervading spirit of irreligion; but not in that true science which had passed beyond the superficial into the profound.

So far from science being irreligious, as many think, it is the neglect of science that is irreligious—it is the refusal to study the surrounding creation that is irreligious. Devotion to science, is a tacit worship—a tacit recognition of worth in the things studied; and by implication in their Cause. It is not a mere lip-homage, but a homage expressed in actions—not a mere professed respect, but a respect proved by the sacrifice of time, thought, and labour.

Nor is it thus only that true science is essentially religious. It is religious, too, inasmuch as it generates a profound respect for, and an implicit faith in, those uniformities of action which all things disclose. By accumulated experiences the man of science acquires a thorough belief in the unchanging relations of phenomena—in the invariable connection of cause and consequence—in the necessity of good or evil results. Instead of the rewards and punishments of traditional belief, which people vaguely hope they may gain, or escape, spite of their disobedience; he finds that there are rewards and punishments in the ordained constitution of things; and that the evil results of disobedience are inevitable. He sees that the laws to which we must submit are both inexorable and beneficent. He sees that in conforming to them, the process of things is ever towards a greater perfection and a higher happiness. Hence he is led constantly to insist on them, and is indignant when they are disregarded. And thus does he, by asserting the eternal principles of things and the necessity of obeying them, prove himself intrinsically religious.

Add lastly the further religious aspect of science, that it alone can give us true conceptions of ourselves and our relation to the mysteries of existence. At the same time that it shows us all which can be known, it shows us the limits beyond which we can know nothing. Not by dogmatic assertion, does it teach the impossibility of comprehending the Ultimate Cause of things; but it leads us clearly to recognise this impossibility by bringing us in every direction to boundaries we cannot cross. It realises to us in a way which nothing else can, the littleness of human intelligence in the face of that which transcends human intelligence.

Thus to the question we set out with—What knowledge is of most worth?—the uniform reply is—Science. This is the verdict on all the counts. For direct self-preservation, or the maintenance of life and health, the all-important knowledge is—Science. For that indirect self-preservation which we call gaining a livelihood, the knowledge of greatest value is—Science. For the due discharge of parental functions, the proper guidance is to be found only in—Science. For that interpretation of national life, past and present, without which the citizen cannot rightly regulate his conduct, the indispensable key is—Science. Alike for the most perfect production and highest enjoyment of art in all its forms, the needful preparation is still—Science. And for purposes of discipline—intellectual, moral, religious—the most efficient study is, once more—Science.

And yet this study, immensely transcending all other in importance, is that which, in an age of boasted education, receives the least attention. While what we call civilisation could never have arisen had it not been for science, science forms scarcely an appreciable element in our so-called civilised training. Though to the progress of science we owe it, that millions find support where once there was food only for thousands; yet of these millions but a few thousand pay any respect to that which has made their existence possible. Though increasing knowledge of the properties and relations of things has not only enabled wandering tribes to grow into populous nations, but has given to the countless members of these populous nations, comforts and pleasures which their few naked ancestors never even conceived, or could have believed, yet is this kind of knowledge only now receiving a grudging recognition in our highest educational institutions. To the slowly growing acquaintance with the uniform co-existences and sequences of phenomena—to the establishment of invariable laws, we owe our emancipation from the grossest superstitions. But for science we should be still worshipping fetishes; or, with hecatombs of victims, propitiating diabolical deities. And yet this science, which, in place of the most degrading conceptions of things, has given us some insight into the grandeurs of creation, is written against in our theologies and frowned upon from our pulpits.

Paraphrasing an Eastern fable, we may say that in the family of knowledges, Science is the household drudge, who, in obscurity, hides unrecognised perfections. To her has been committed all the works; by her skill, intelligence, and devotion, have all conveniences and gratifications been obtained; and while ceaselessly ministering to the rest, she has been kept in the background, that her haughty sisters might flaunt their fripperies in the eyes of the world. The parallel holds yet further. For we are fast coming to the *dénouement,* when the positions will be changed; and while these haughty sisters sink into merited neglect, Science, proclaimed as highest alike in worth and beauty, will reign supreme.

6. Intellectual Education*

"Intellectual Education" formed the second chapter of Education: Intellectual, Moral and Physical *(1860 and 1861). It was the first of Spencer's separate essays on education, and it originally appeared in* The North British Review *(May, 1854) under the title "The Art of Education." Spencer's own title was "Method in Education."*

The article was ostensibly a review of several books dealing with pedagogical questions: C. Marcel's Language as a Means of Mental Culture and International Communication, *Thomas Wyse's* Education Reform, *James Pillan's* Principles of Elementary Teaching, *E. Biber's* Life of Pestalozzi, *etc. Spencer himself later recounted that the topic had a "triple interest" for him: It had "direct connexions with psychology, which was at that time dominant in my thoughts"; it related to "certain results of observation, and to some extent of experiment, which seemed worth setting forth, considered intrinsically"; and it served to illustrate and elucidate the place of mental development "in the theory of development at large." In enunciating and elaborating the principles of education as a process of "self-instruction" and, consequently, as one of "pleasurable instruction," Spencer recognized "the direct influence" of his father.† It is obvious, of course, that Spencer was influenced by other contemporary educational writers.*

* *Essays on Education, Etc.* (London: J. M. Dent and Sons, Ltd., 1911), pp. 51–83. Abridged.

† *Autobiography,* I, 506–509.

. . . But of all the changes taking place, the most significant is the growing desire to make the acquirement of knowledge pleasurable rather than painful—a desire based on the more or less distinct perception, that at each age the intellectual action which a child likes is a healthful one for it; and conversely. There is a spreading opinion that the rise of an appetite for any kind of information implies that the unfolding mind has become fit to assimilate it, and needs it for purposes of growth; and that, on the other hand, the disgust felt towards such information is a sign either that it is prematurely presented, or that it is presented in an indigestible form. Hence the efforts to make early education amusing, and all education interesting.

What now is the common characteristic of these several changes? Is it not an increasing conformity to the methods of Nature? The relinquishment of early forcing, against which Nature rebels, and the leaving of the first years for exercise of the limbs and senses, show this. The superseding of rote-learnt lessons by lessons orally and experimentally given, like those of the field and playground, shows this. The disuse of rule-teaching, and the adoption of teaching by principles—that is, the leaving of generalisations until there are particulars to base them on—show this. The system of object-lessons shows this. The teaching of the rudiments of science in the concrete instead of the abstract, shows this. And above all, this tendency is shown in the variously-directed efforts to present knowledge in attractive forms, and so to make the acquirement of it pleasurable. For, as it is the order of Nature in all creatures that the gratification accompanying the fulfilment of needful functions serves as a stimulus to their fulfilment—as, during the self-education of the young child, the delight taken in the biting of corals and the pulling to pieces of toys, becomes the prompter to actions which teach it the properties of matter; it follows that, in choosing the succession of subjects and the modes of instruction which most interest the pupil, we are fulfilling Nature's behests, and adjusting our proceedings to the laws of life.

Thus, then, we are on the highway towards the doctrine long ago enunciated by Pestalozzi, that alike in its order and its methods, education must conform to the natural process of mental evolution—that there is a certain sequence in which the faculties spontaneously develop, and a certain kind of knowledge which each requires during its development; and that it is for us to ascertain this sequence, and supply this knowledge. All the improvements above alluded to are partial applications of this general principle.

"But why trouble ourselves about any *curriculum* at all?" it may be asked. "If it be true that the mind like the body has a predetermined course of evolution—if it unfolds spontaneously—if its successive desires for this or that kind of information arise when these are severally required for its nutrition—if there thus exists in itself a prompter to the right species of activity at the right time; why interfere in any way? Why not leave children *wholly* to the discipline of nature?—why not remain quite passive and let them get knowledge as they best can?—why not be consistent throughout?" This is an awkward-looking question. Plausibly implying as it does, that a system of complete *laissez-faire* is the logical outcome of the doctrines set forth, it seems to furnish a disproof of them by *reductio ad absurdum*. In truth, however, they do not, when rightly understood, commit us to any such untenable position. A glance at the physical analogies will clearly show this. It is a general law of life that the more complex the organism to be produced, the longer the period during which it is dependent on a parent organism for food and protection. The difference between the minute, rapidly-formed, and self-moving spore of a conferva, and the slowly-developed seed of a tree, with its multiplied envelopes and large stock of nutriment laid by to nourish the germ during its first stages of growth, illustrates this law in its application to the vegetal world. Among animals we may trace it in a series of contrasts from the monad whose spontaneously-divided halves are as self-sufficing the moment after their separation as was the original whole; up to man, whose offspring not only passes through a protracted gestation, and subsequently long depends on the breast for sustenance; but after that must have its food artificially administered; must, when it has learned to feed itself, continue to have bread, clothing, and shelter provided; and does not acquire the power of complete self-support until a time varying from fifteen to twenty years after its birth. Now this law applies to the mind as to the body. For mental pabulum also, every higher creature, and especially man, is at first dependent on adult aid. Lacking the ability to move about, the babe is almost as powerless to get materials on which to exercise its perceptions as it is to get supplies for its stomach. Unable to prepare its own food, it is in like manner unable to reduce many kinds of knowledge to a fit form for assimilation. The language through which all higher truths are to be gained, it wholly derives from those surrounding it. And we see in such an example as the Wild Boy of Aveyron, the arrest of development that results when no help is received from parents and nurses. Thus, in providing from day to day the right kind of facts, prepared in the right manner, and giving them in due abundance at appropriate intervals, there is as much scope for active ministration to a child's mind as to its body. In either case, it is the chief function of parents to see that the *conditions* requisite to growth are maintained. And as, in supplying aliment, and clothing, and shelter, they may fulfil this function without at all interfering with the spontaneous development of the limbs and viscera, either in their order or mode; so, they may supply sounds for imitation, objects for examination, books for reading, problems for solution, and, if they use neither direct nor indirect coercion, may do this without in any way disturbing the normal process of mental evolution; or rather, may greatly facilitate that process. Hence the admission of the doctrines enunciated does not, as some might argue, involve the abandonment of teaching; but leaves ample room for an active and elaborate course of culture.

Passing from generalities to special considerations, it is to be remarked that in practice the Pestalozzian system seems scarcely to have fulfilled the promise of its theory. While, therefore, we would defend in its entire extent the general doctrine which Pestalozzi inaugurated, we think great evil likely to result from an uncritical reception of his specific methods. That tendency, constantly exhibited by mankind, to canonise the forms and practices along with which any great truth has been bequeathed to them—their liability to prostrate their intellects before the prophet, and swear by his every word— their proneness to mistake the clothing of the idea for the idea itself; renders it needful to insist strongly upon the distinction between the fundamental principle of the Pestalozzian system, and the set of expedients devised for its practice; and to suggest that while the one may be considered as established, the other is probably nothing but an adumbration of the normal course. Indeed, on looking at the state of our knowledge, we may be quite sure that is the case. Before educational methods can be made to harmonise in character and arrangement with the faculties in their mode and order of unfolding, it is first needful that we ascertain with some completeness how the faculties *do* unfold. At present we have acquired, on this point, only a few general notions. These general notions must be developed in detail—must be transformed into a multitude of specific propositions, before we can be said to possess that *science* on which the *art* of education must be based. And then, when we have definitely made out in what succession and in what combinations the mental powers become active, it remains to choose out of the many possible ways of exercising each of them, that which best conforms to its natural mode of action. Evidently, therefore, it is not to be supposed that even our most advanced modes of teaching are the right ones, or nearly the right ones.

Bearing in mind then this distinction between the principle and the practice of Pestalozzi, and inferring from the grounds assigned that the last must necessarily be very defective, the reader will rate at its true worth the dissatisfaction with the system which some have expressed; and will see that the realisation of the Pestalozzian idea remains to be achieved. Should he argue, however, from what has just been said, that no such realisation is at present practicable, and that all effort ought to be devoted to the preliminary inquiry; we reply, that though it is not possible for a scheme of culture to be perfected either in matter or form until a rational psychology has been established, it is possible, with the aid of certain guiding principles, to make empirical approximations towards a perfect scheme. To prepare the way for further research we will now specify these principles.

Some of them have been more or less distinctly implied
in the foregoing pages; but it will be well here to state
them all in logical order.

1. That in education we should proceed from the
simple to the complex, is a truth which has always been
to some extent acted upon: not professedly, indeed, nor
by any means consistently. The mind develops. Like all
things that develop it progresses from the homogeneous
to the heterogeneous; and a normal training system, being an objective counterpart of this subjective process,
must exhibit a like progression. Moreover, thus inter-
preting it, we may see that this formula has much wider
application than at first appears. For its *rationale* involves, not only that we should proceed from the single
to the combined in the teaching of each branch of knowledge; but that we should do the like with knowledge as a
whole. As the mind, consisting at first of but few active
faculties, has its later-completed faculties successively
brought into play, and ultimately comes to have all its
faculties in simultaneous action; it follows that our
teaching should begin with but few subjects at once,
and successively adding to these, should finally carry on
all subjects abreast. Not only in its details should education proceed from the simple to the complex, but in its
ensemble also.

2. The development of the mind, as all other development, is an advance from the indefinite to the definite.
In common with the rest of the organisms, the brain
reaches its finished structure only at maturity; and in
proportion as its structure is unfinished, its actions are
wanting in precision. Hence like the first movements and
the first attempts at speech, the first perceptions and
thoughts are extremely vague. As from a rudimentary
eye, discerning only the difference between light and

darkness, the progress is to an eye that distinguishes kinds and gradations of colour, and details of form, with the greatest exactness; so, the intellect as a whole and in each faculty, beginning with the rudest discriminations among objects and actions, advances towards discriminations of increasing nicety and distinctness. To this general law our educational course and methods must conform.

3. To say that our lessons ought to start from the concrete and end in the abstract, may be considered as in part a repetition of the first of the foregoing principles. Nevertheless it is a maxim that must be stated: if with no other view, then with the view of showing in certain cases what are truly the simple and the complex. For unfortunately there has been much misunderstanding on this point. General formulas which men have devised to express groups of details, and which have severally simplified their conceptions by uniting many facts into one fact, they have supposed must simplify the conceptions of a child also. They have forgotten that a generalisation is simple only in comparison with the whole mass of particular truths it comprehends—that it is more complex than any one of these truths taken singly—that only after many of these single truths have been acquired does the generalisation ease the memory and help the reason— and that to a mind not possessing these single truths it is necessarily a mystery. Thus confounding two kinds of simplification, teachers have constantly erred by setting out with "first principles": a proceeding essentially, though not apparently, at variance with the primary rule; which implies that the mind should be introduced to principles through the medium of examples, and so should be led from the particular to the general—from the concrete to the abstract.

4.   The education of the child must accord both in mode and arrangement with the education of mankind, considered historically. In other words, the genesis of knowledge in the individual must follow the same course as the genesis of knowledge in the race. In strictness, this principle may be considered as already expressed by implication; since both, being processes of evolution, must conform to those same general laws of evolution above insisted on, and must therefore agree with each other. Nevertheless this particular parallelism is of value for the specific guidance it affords. To M. Comte we believe society owes the enunciation of it; and we may accept this item of his philosophy without at all committing ourselves to the rest. This doctrine may be upheld by two reasons, quite independent of any abstract theory; and either of them sufficient to establish it. One is deducible from the law of hereditary transmission as considered in its wider consequences. For if it be true that men exhibit likeness to ancestry, both in aspect and character—if it be true that certain mental manifestations, as insanity, occur in successive members of the same family at the same age—if, passing from individual cases in which the traits of many dead ancestors mixing with those of a few living ones greatly obscure the law, we turn to national types, and remark how the contrasts between them are persistent from age to age—if we remember that these respective types came from a common stock, and that hence the present marked differences between them must have arisen from the action of modifying circumstances upon successive generations who severally transmitted the accumulated effects to their descendants—if we find the differences to be now organic, so that a French child grows into a French man even when brought up among strangers—and if the general

fact thus illustrated is true of the whole nature, intellect inclusive; then it follows that if there be an order in which the human race has mastered its various kinds of knowledge, there will arise in every child an aptitude to acquire these kinds of knowledge in the same order. So that even were the order intrinsically indifferent, it would facilitate education to lead the individual mind through the steps traversed by the general mind. But the order is *not* intrinsically indifferent; and hence the fundamental reason why education should be a repetition of civilisation in little. It is provable both that the historical sequence was, in its main outlines, a necessary one; and that the causes which determined it apply to the child as to the race. Not to specify these causes in detail, it will suffice here to point out that as the mind of humanity placed in the midst of phenomena and striving to comprehend them, has, after endless comparisons, speculations, experiments, and theories, reached its present knowledge of each subject by a specific route; it may rationally be inferred that the relationship between mind and phenomena is such as to prevent this knowledge from being reached by any other route; and that as each child's mind stands in this same relationship to phenomena, they can be accessible to it only through the same route. Hence in deciding upon the right method of education, an inquiry into the method of civilisation will help to guide us.

5. One of the conclusions to which such an inquiry leads, is, that in each branch of instruction we should proceed from the empirical to the rational. During human progress, every science is evolved out of its corresponding art. It results from the necessity we are under, both individually and as a race, of reaching the abstract by way of the concrete, that there must be practice and

an accruing experience with its empirical generalisation, before there can be science. Science is organised knowledge; and before knowledge can be organised, some of it must be possessed. Every study, therefore, should have a purely experimental introduction; and only after an ample fund of observations has been accumulated, should reasoning begin. As illustrative applications of this rule, we may instance the modern course of placing grammar, not before language, but after it; or the ordinary custom of prefacing perspective by practical drawing. By and by further applications of it will be indicated.

6. A second corollary from the foregoing general principle, and one which cannot be too strenuously insisted on, is, that in education the process of self-development should be encouraged to the uttermost. Children should be led to make their own investigations, and to draw their own inferences. They should be *told* as little as possible, and induced to *discover* as much as possible. Humanity has progressed solely by self-instruction; and that to achieve the best results, each mind must progress somewhat after the same fashion, is continually proved by the marked success of self-made men.

7. As a final test by which to judge any plan of culture, should come the question,—Does it create a pleasurable excitement in the pupils? When in doubt whether a particular mode or arrangement is or is not more in harmony with the foregoing principles than some other, we may safely abide by this criterion. Even when, as considered theoretically, the proposed course seems the best, yet if it produces no interest, or less interest than some other course, we should relinquish it; for a child's intellectual instincts are more trustworthy than our reasonings. In respect to the knowing-faculties, we may

confidently trust in the general law, that under normal conditions, healthful action is pleasurable, while action which gives pain is not healthful. Though at present very incompletely conformed to by the emotional nature, yet by the intellectual nature, or at least by those parts of it which the child exhibits, this law is almost wholly conformed to. The repugnances to this and that study which vex the ordinary teacher, are not innate, but result from his unwise system.

With most, these guiding principles will weigh but little if left in this abstract form. Partly, therefore, to exemplify their application, and partly with a view of making sundry specific suggestions, we propose now to pass from the theory of education to the practice of it.

It was the opinion of Pestalozzi, and one which has ever since his day been gaining ground, that education of some kind should begin from the cradle. Whoever has watched, with any discernment, the wide-eyed gaze of the infant at surrounding objects knows very well that education *does* begin thus early, whether we intend it or not; and that these fingerings and suckings of everything it can lay hold of, these open-mouthed listenings to every sound, are first steps in the series which ends in the discovery of unseen planets, the invention of calculating engines, the production of great paintings, or the composition of symphonies and operas. This activity of the faculties from the very first, being spontaneous and inevitable, the question is whether we shall supply in due variety the materials on which they may exercise themselves; and to the question so put, none but an affirmative answer can be given.

Joining this with the suggestions for "a nursery method," set down in his *Mother's Manual,* in which he makes the names, positions, connections, numbers, properties, and uses of the limbs and body his first lessons, it becomes clear that Pestalozzi's notions on early mental development were too crude to enable him to devise judicious plans. Let us consider the course which Psychology dictates.

The earliest impressions which the mind can assimilate are the undecomposable sensations produced by resistance, light, sound, etc. Following, therefore, the necessary law of progression from the simple to the complex, we should provide for the infant a sufficiency of objects presenting different degrees and kinds of resistance, a sufficiency of objects reflecting different amounts and qualities of light, and a sufficiency of sounds contrasted in their loudness, their pitch and their *timbre*. How fully this *à priori* conclusion is confirmed by infantile instincts, all will see on being reminded of the delight which every young child has in biting its toys, in feeling its brother's bright jacket-buttons, and pulling papa's whiskers— how absorbed it becomes in gazing at any gaudily-painted object, to which it applies the word "pretty," when it can pronounce it, wholly because of the bright colours— and how its face broadens into a laugh at the tattlings of its nurse, the snapping of a visitor's fingers, or any sound which it has not before heard.

We are quite prepared to hear from many that all this is throwing away time and energy; and that children would be much better occupied in writing their copies or learning their pence-tables, and so fitting themselves for the business of life. We regret that such crude ideas of what constitutes education, and such a narrow conception of utility, should still be prevalent. Saying nothing on the need for a systematic culture of the perceptions and the value of the practices above inculcated as subserving that need, we are prepared to defend them even on the score of the knowledge gained. If men are to be mere cits, mere porers over ledgers, with no ideas beyond their trades—if it is well that they should be as the cockney whose conception of rural pleasures extends no further than sitting in a tea-garden smoking pipes and drinking porter; or as the squire who thinks of woods as places for shooting in, of uncultivated plants as nothing but weeds, and who classifies animals into game, vermin, and stock—then indeed it is needless to learn anything that does not directly help to replenish the till and fill the larder. But if there is a more worthy aim for us than to be drudges—if there are other uses in the things around than their power to bring money—if there are higher faculties to be exercised than acquisitive and sensual ones—if the pleasures which poetry and art and science and philosophy can bring are of any moment; than is it desirable that the instinctive inclination which every child shows to observe natural beauties and investigate natural phenomena, should be encouraged. But this gross utilitarianism which is content to come into the world and quit it again without knowing what kind of a world it is or what it contains, may be met on its own ground. It will by and by be found that a knowledge of the laws of life is more important than any other knowledge whatever—that the laws of life underlie not only all bodily and mental processes, but by implication all the transactions of the house and the street, all commerce, all politics, all morals—and that therefore without a comprehension of them, neither personal nor social conduct can be rightly regulated. It will eventually be seen too, that the laws of life are essentially the same throughout the whole organic creation; and further, that they cannot be properly understood in their complex manifestations until they have been studied in their simpler ones. And when this is seen, it will be also seen that in aiding the child to acquire the out-of-door information for which it shows so great an avidity, and in encouraging the acquisition of such information throughout youth, we are simply inducing it to store up the raw material for future organisation—the facts that will one day bring home to it with due force, those great generalisations of science by which actions may be rightly guided.

The spreading recognition of drawing as an element of education is one among many signs of the more rational views on mental culture now beginning to prevail. Once more it may be remarked that teachers are at length adopting the course which Nature has perpetually been pressing on their notice. The spontaneous attempts made by children to represent the men, houses, trees, and animals around them—on a slate if they can get nothing better, or with lead-pencil on paper if they can beg them —are familiar to all. To be shown through a picture-book is one of their highest gratifications; and as usual, their strong imitative tendency presently generates in them the ambition to make pictures themselves also. This effort to depict the striking things they see is a further instinctive exercise of the perceptions—a means whereby still greater accuracy and completeness of observation are induced. And alike by trying to interest us in their discoveries of the sensible properties of things, and by their endeavours to draw, they solicit from us just that kind of culture which they most need.

Had teachers been guided by Nature's hints, not only in making drawing a part of education but in choosing modes of teaching it, they would have done still better than they have done. What is that the child first tries to represent? Things that are large, things that are attractive in colour, things round which its pleasurable associations most cluster—human beings from whom it has received so many emotions; cows and dogs which interest by the many phenomena they present; houses that are hourly visible and strike by their size and contrast of parts. And which of the processes of representation gives it most delight? Colouring. Paper and pencil are good in default of something better; but a box of paints and a brush—these are the treasures. The extreme indefiniteness which, in conformity with the law of evolution, these first attempts exhibit, is anything but a reason for ignoring them. No matter how grotesque the shapes produced; no matter how daubed and glaring the colours. The question is not whether the child is producing good drawings. The question is, whether it is developing its faculties. It has first to gain some command over its fingers, some crude notions of likeness; and this practice is better than any other for these ends, since it is the spontaneous and interesting one. During early childhood no formal drawing-lessons are possible. Shall we therefore repress, or neglect to aid, these efforts at self-culture? or shall we encourage and guide them as normal exercises of the perceptions and the powers of manipulation? If by furnishing cheap woodcuts to be painted, and simple contour-maps to have their boundary lines tinted, we can not only pleasurably draw out the faculty of colour, but can incidentally produce some familiarity with the outlines of things and countries, and some ability to move the brush steadily; and if by the supply of tempting objects we can keep up the instinctive practice of making representations, however rough; it must happen that when the age for lessons in drawing is reached, there will exist a facility that would else have been absent. Time will have been gained; and trouble, both to teacher and pupil, saved.

From what has been said, it may be readily inferred

that we condemn the practice of drawing from copies; and still more so that formal discipline in making straight lines and curved lines and compound lines, with which it is the fashion of some teachers to begin. It has been well said concerning the custom of prefacing the art of speaking any tongue by a drilling in the parts of speech and their functions, that it is about as reasonable as prefacing the art of walking by a course of lessons on the bones, muscles, and nerves of the legs; and much the same thing may be said of the proposal to preface the art of representing objects, by a nomenclature and definitions of the lines which they yield on analysis. These technicalities are alike repulsive and needless. They render the study distasteful at the very outset; and all with the view of teaching that which, in the course of practice, will be learnt unconsciously. Just as the child incidentally gathers the meanings of ordinary words from the conversations going on around it, without the help of dictionaries; so, from the remarks on objects, pictures, and its own drawings, will it presently acquire, not only without effort but even pleasurably, those same scientific terms which, when taught at first, are a mystery and a weariness.

If any dependence is to be placed on the general principles of education that have been laid down, the process of learning to draw should be throughout continuous with those efforts of early childhood, described above as so worthy of encouragement. By the time that the voluntary practice thus initiated has given some steadiness of hand, and some tolerable ideas of proportion, there will have arisen a vague notion of body as presenting its three dimensions in perspective. And when, after sundry abortive, Chinese-like attempts to render this appearance on paper, there has grown up a pretty clear perception of the thing to be done, and a desire to do it, a first lesson in empirical perspective may be given by means of the apparatus occasionally used in explaining perspective as a science. Thus, without the unintelligent, mechanical practice of copying other drawings, but by a method at once simple and attractive—rational, yet not abstract—a familiarity with the linear appearances of things, and a faculty of rendering them, may be step by step acquired. To which advantages add these:— that even thus early the pupil learns, almost unconsciously, the true theory of a picture (namely, that it is a delineation of objects as they appear when projected on a plane placed between them and the eye); and that when he reaches a fit age for commencing scientific perspective, he is already thoroughly acquainted with the facts which form its logical basis.

To continue these suggestions much further, would be to write a detailed treatise on education, which we do not purpose. The foregoing outlines of plans for exercising the perceptions in early childhood, for conducting object-lessons, for teaching drawing and geometry, must be considered simply as illustrations of the method dictated by the general principles previously specified. We believe that on examination they will be found not only to progress from the simple to the complex, from the indefinite to the definite, from the concrete to the abstract, from the empirical to the rational; but to satisfy the further requirements, that education shall be a repetition of civilisation in little, that it shall be as much as possible a process of self-evolution, and that it shall be pleasurable. The fulfilment of all these conditions by one type of method, tends alike to verify the conditions, and to prove that type of the method the right one. Mark too, that this method is the logical outcome of the ten-

dency characterising all modern improvements in tuition
—that it is but an adoption in full of the natural system
which they adopt partially—that it displays this complete
adoption of the natural system, both by conforming to the
above principles, and by following the suggestions which
the unfolding mind itself gives: facilitating its spontaneous activities, and so aiding the developments which
Nature is busy with. Thus there seems abundant reason
to conclude, that the mode of procedure above exemplified, closely approximates to the true one.

A few paragraphs must be added in further inculcation
of the two general principles, that are alike the most
important and the least attended to; namely, the principle that throughout youth, as in early childhood and in
maturity, the process shall be one of self-instruction; and
the obverse principle, that the mental action induced
shall be throughout intrinsically grateful. If progression
from simple to complex, from indefinite to definite, and
from concrete to abstract, be considered the essential requirements as dictated by abstract psychology; then do
the requirements that knowledge shall be self-mastered,
and pleasurably mastered, become tests by which we
may judge whether the dictates of abstract psychology
are being obeyed. If the first embody the leading generalisations of the *science* of mental growth, the last are the
chief canons of the *art* of fostering mental growth. For
manifestly, if the steps in our *curriculum* are so arranged
that they can be successively ascended by the pupil himself with little or no help, they must correspond with
the stages of evolution in his faculties; and manifestly, if
the successive achievements of these steps are intrinsically gratifying to him, it follows that they require no
more than a normal exercise of his powers.

But making education a process of self-evolution, has

other advantages than this of keeping our lessons in the right order. In the first place, it guarantees a vividness and permanency of impression which the usual methods can never produce. Any piece of knowledge which the pupil has himself acquired—any problem which he has himself solved, becomes, by virtue of the conquest, much more thoroughly his than it could else be. The preliminary activity of mind which his success implies, the concentration of thought necessary to it, and the excitement consequent on his triumph, conspire to register the facts in his memory in a way that no mere information heard from a teacher, or read in a school-book, can be registered. Even if he fails, the tension to which his faculties have been wound up, insures his remembrance of the solution when given to him, better than half-a-dozen repetitions would. Observe, again, that this discipline necessitates a continuous organisation of the knowledge he acquires. It is in the very nature of facts and inferences assimilated in this normal manner, that they successively become the premises of further conclusions— the means of solving further questions. The solution of yesterday's problem helps the pupil in mastering to-day's. Thus the knowledge is turned into faculty as soon as it is taken in, and forthwith aids in the general function of thinking—does not lie merely written on the pages of an internal library, as when rote-learnt. Mark further, the moral culture which this constant self-help involves. Courage in attacking difficulties, patient concentration of the attention, perseverance through failures—these are characteristics which after-life specially requires; and these are characteristics which this system of making the mind work for its food specially produces. That it is thoroughly practicable to carry out instruction after this fashion, we can ourselves testify; having been in youth thus led to solve the comparatively complex problems of perspective. And that leading teachers have been tending in this direction, is indicated alike in the saying of Fellenberg, that "the individual, independent activity of the pupil is of much greater importance than the ordinary busy officiousness of many who assume the office of educators;" in the opinion of Horace Mann, that "unfortunately education amongst us at present consists too much in *telling*, not in *training*;" and in the remark of M. Marcel, that "what the learner discovers by mental exertion is better known than what is told to him."

Similarly with the correlative requirement, that the method of culture pursued shall be one productive of an intrinsically happy activity,—an activity not happy because of extrinsic rewards to be obtained, but because of its own healthfulness. Conformity to this requirement, besides preventing us from thwarting the normal process of evolution, incidentally secures positive benefits of importance. Unless we are to return to an ascetic morality (or rather *im*-morality) the maintenance of youthful happiness must be considered as in itself a worthy aim. Not to dwell upon this, however, we go on to remark that a pleasurable state of feeling is far more favourable to intellectual action than a state of indifference or disgust. Every one knows that things read, heard, or seen with interest, are better remembered than things read, heard, or seen with apathy. In the one case the faculties appealed to are actively occupied with the subject presented; in the other they are inactively occupied with it, and the attention is continually drawn away by more attractive thoughts. Hence the impressions are respectively strong and weak. Moreover, to the intellectual listlessness which a pupil's lack of interest in any study involves, must be added the paralysing fear of consequences.

This, by distracting his attention, increases the difficulty he finds in bringing his faculties to bear upon facts that are repugnant to them. Clearly, therefore, the efficiency of tuition will, other things equal, be proportionate to the gratification with which tasks are performed.

It should be considered also, that grave moral consequences depend upon the habitual pleasure or pain which daily lessons produce.

There remains yet another indirect result of no small moment. The relationship between teachers and their pupils is, other things equal, rendered friendly and influential, or antagonistic and powerless, according as the system of culture produces happiness or misery. Human beings are at the mercy of their associated ideas. A daily minister of pain cannot fail to be regarded with secret dislike; and if he causes no emotions but painful ones, will inevitably be hated. Conversely, he who constantly aids children to their ends, hourly provides them with the satisfactions of conquest, hourly encourages them through their difficulties and sympathises in their successes, will be liked; nay, if his behaviour is consistent throughout, must be loved. And when we remember how efficient and benign is the control of a master who is felt to be a friend, when compared with the control of one who is looked upon with aversion, or at best indifference, we may infer that the indirect advantages of conducting education on the happiness principle do not fall far short of the direct ones. To all who question the possibility of acting out the system here advocated, we reply as before, that not only does theory point to it, but experience commends it.

As suggesting a final reason for making education a process of self-instruction, and by consequence a process

of pleasurable instruction, we may advert to the fact
that, in proportion as it is made so, is there a probability
that it will not cease when schooldays end. As long as the
acquisition of knowledge is rendered habitually repugnant, so long will there be a prevailing tendency to dis-
continue it when free from the coercion of parents and
masters. And when the acquisition of knowledge has been
rendered habitually gratifying, then will there be as
prevailing a tendency to continue, without superintendence, that self-culture previously carried on under superintendence. These results are inevitable. While the laws
of mental association remain true—while men dislike the
things and places that suggest painful recollections, and
delight in those which call to mind bygone pleasures—
painful lessons will make knowledge repulsive, and
pleasurable lessons will make it attractive. The men to
whom in boyhood information came in dreary tasks along
with threats of punishment, and who were never led into
habits of independent inquiry, are unlikely to be students
in after years; while those to whom it came in the natural
forms, at the proper times, and who remember its facts
as not only interesting in themselves, but as the occasions
of a long series of gratifying successes, are likely to continue through life that self-instruction commenced in
youth.

7. On Science as Discipline*

In the midst of his vast project—the synthetic philosophy —Spencer was persuaded by E. L. Youmans, his "American friend," to write an "extra" volume. The result was The Study of Sociology, *one of the most popular and widely-read of Spencer's books. It first appeared in 1872 in the form of articles for the* Contemporary Review *and for Youmans' newly-established* Popular Science Monthly. *It was first published as a separate volume in 1873, and it reappeared in several editions thereafter. Interestingly, it has recently been reissued in the United States as a paperback, with an introduction by Talcott Parsons. Some of Parsons' comments are worthy of quoting because they reveal a sympathetic view of Spencer's sociology among modern American sociologists. Although Parsons quickly points out that Spencer's book contains "much that is dated and that reflects the particularities of the man and his time," nevertheless, it also contains "much that is surprisingly modern and relevant to our own time." Parsons continues: "It may be said that Spencer's thinking about society is informed with three main basic positive theoretical ideas: first, that of society as a self-regulating system, second, that of differentiation of function, and third, that of evolution, all of which remain as important today as they were when he wrote."†*

* *The Study of Sociology* (New York: D. Appleton and Co., 1896), pp. 316–326.

† From the introduction by Talcott Parsons to Herbert Spencer, *The Study of Sociology* (Ann Arbor: The University of Michigan Press, 1961), pp. v–vi.

A fit habit of thought, then, is all-important in the study of Sociology; and a fit habit of thought can be acquired only by study of the Sciences at large. For Sociology is a science in which the phenomena of all other sciences are included. It presents those necessities of relation with which the Abstract Sciences deal; it presents those connexions of cause and effect which the Abstract-Concrete Sciences familiarize the student with; and it presents that concurrence of many causes and production of contingent results, which the Concrete Sciences show us, but which we are shown especially by the organic sciences. Hence, to acquire the habit of thought conducive to right thinking in Sociology, the mind must be familiarized with the fundamental ideas which each class of sciences brings into view; and must not be possessed by those of any one class, or any two classes, of sciences.

That this may be better seen, let me briefly indicate the indispensable discipline which each class of sciences gives to the intellect; and also the wrong intellectual habits produced if that class of sciences is studied exclusively.

Entire absence of training in the Abstract Sciences, leaves the mind without due sense of *necessity of relation*. Watch the mental movements of the wholly-ignorant, before whom there have been brought not even those exact and fixed connexions which Arithmetic exhibits, and it will be seen that they have nothing like irresistible convictions that from given data there is an inevitable inference. That which to you has the aspect of a certainty, seems to them not free from doubt. Even men whose educations have made numerical processes and results tolerably familiar, will show in a case where the implication is logical only, that they have not absolute confidence in the dependence of conclusion on premisses.

Unshakeable beliefs in necessities of relation, are to be gained only by studying the Abstract Sciences, Logic and Mathematics. Dealing with necessities of relation of the simplest class, Logic is of some service to this end; though often of less service than it might be, for the reason that the symbols used are not translated into thoughts, and hence the connexions stated are not really represented. Only when, for a logical implication expressed in the abstract, there is substituted an example so far concrete that the inter-dependencies can be contemplated, is there an exercise of the mental power by which logical necessity is grasped. Of the discipline given by Mathematics, also, it is to be remarked that the habit of dealing with necessities of numerical relation, though in a degree useful for cultivating the consciousness of necessity, is not in a high degree useful; because, in the immense majority of cases, the mind, occupied with the symbols used, and not passing beyond them to the groups of units they stand for, does not really figure to itself the relations expressed—does not really discern their necessities; and has not therefore the conception of necessity perpetually repeated. It is the more special division of Mathematics, dealing with Space-relations, which above all other studies yields necessary ideas; and so makes strong and definite the consciousness of necessity in general. A geometrical demonstration time after time presents premisses and conclusion in such wise that the relation alleged is seen in thought—cannot be passed over by mere symbolization. Each step exhibits some connexion of positions or quantities as one that could not be otherwise; and hence the habit of taking such steps makes the consciousness of such connexions familiar and vivid.

But while mathematical discipline, and especially discipline in Geometry, is extremely useful if not indispensable, as a means of preparing the mind to recognize throughout Nature the absoluteness of uniformities; it is, if exclusively or too-habitually pursued, apt to produce perversions of general thought. Inevitably it establishes a special bent of mind; and inevitably this special bent affects all the intellectual actions—causes a tendency to look in a mathematical way at matters beyond the range of Mathematics. The mathematician is ever dealing with phenomena of which the elements are relatively few and definite. His most involved problem is immeasurably less involved than are the problems of the Concrete Sciences. But, when considering these, he cannot help thinking after his habitual way: in dealing with questions which the Concrete Sciences present, he recognizes some few only of the factors, tacitly ascribes to these a definiteness which they have not, and proceeds after the mathematical manner to draw positive conclusions from these data, as though they were specific and adequate.

Hence the truth, so often illustrated, that mathematicians are bad reasoners on contingent matters. To older illustrations may be added the recent one yielded by M. Michel Chasles, who proved himself incapable as a judge of evidence in the matter of the Newton-Pascal forgeries. Another was supplied by the late Professor De Morgan, who, bringing his mental eye to bear with microscopic power on some small part of a question, ignored its main features.

By cultivation of the Abstract-Concrete Sciences, there is produced a further habit of thought, not otherwise produced, which is essential to right thinking in general; and, by implication, to right thinking in Sociology. Familiarity with the various orders of physical and chemical phenomena, gives distinctness and strength to the consciousness of *cause and effect*.

Experiences of things around do, indeed, yield conceptions of special forces and of force in general. The uncultured get from these experiences, degrees of faith in causation such that where they see some striking effect they usually assume an adequate cause, and where a cause of given amount is manifest, a proportionate effect is looked for. Especially is this so where the actions are simple mechanical actions. Still, these impressions which daily life furnishes, if unaided by those derived from physical science, leave the mind with but vague ideas of causal relations. It needs but to remember the readiness with which people accept the alleged facts of the Spiritualists, many of which imply a direct negation of the mechanical axiom that action and reaction are equal and opposite, to see how much the ordinary thoughts of causation lack quantitativeness—lack the idea of proportion between amount of force expended and amount of change wrought. Very generally, too, the ordinary thoughts of causation are not even qualitatively valid: the most absurd notions as to what cause will produce what effect are frequently disclosed. Take, for instance, the popular belief that a goat kept in a stable will preserve the health of the horses; and note how this belief, accepted on the authority of grooms and coachmen, is repeated by their educated employers—as I lately heard it repeated by an American general, and agreed in by two retired English officials. Clearly, the readiness to admit, on such evidence, that such a cause can produce such an effect, implies a consciousness of causation which, even qualitatively considered, is of the crudest kind. And such a consciousness is, indeed, everywhere betrayed by the superstitions traceable among all classes.

Hence we must infer that the uncompared and unanalyzed observations men make in the course of their dealings with things around, do not suffice to give them wholly-rational ideas of the process of things. It requires that physical actions shall be critically examined, the factors and results measured, and different cases contrasted, before there can be reached clear ideas of necessary causal dependence. And thus to investigate physical actions is the business of the Abstract-Concrete Sciences. Every experiment which the physicist or the chemist makes, brings afresh before his consciousness the truth, given countless times in his previous experiences, that from certain antecedents of particular kinds there will inevitably follow a particular kind of consequent; and that from certain amounts of the antecedents, the amount of the consequent will be inevitably so much. The habit of thought generated by these hourly-repeated experiences, always the same, always exact, is one which makes it impossible to think of any effect as arising without a cause, or any cause as expended without an effect; and one which makes it impossible to think of an effect out of proportion to its cause, or a cause out of proportion to its effect.

While, however, study of the Abstract-Concrete Sciences carried on experimentally, gives clearness and strength to the consciousness of causation, taken alone it is inadequate as a discipline; and if pursued exclusively, it generates a habit of thought which betrays into erroneous conclusions when higher orders of phenomena are dealt with. The process of physical inquiry is essentially analytical; and the daily pursuit of this process generates two tendencies—the tendency to contemplate singly those factors which it is the aim to disentangle and identify and measure; and the tendency to rest in the results reached, as though they were the final results to be sought. The chemist, by saturating, neutralizing, decom-

posing, precipitating, and at last separating, is enabled to
measure what quantity of this element had been held
in combination by a given quantity of that; and when,
by some alternative course of analysis, he has verified
the result, his inquiry is in so far concluded: as are kindred inquiries respecting other affinities of the element,
when these are qualitatively and quantitatively determined. His habit is to get rid of, or neglect as much as
possible, the concomitant disturbing factors, that he
may ascertain the nature and amount of some one, and
then of some other and his end is achieved when accounts have been given of all the factors, individually
considered. So is it, too, with the physicist. Say the
problem is the propagation of sound through air, and
the interpretation of its velocity—say, that the velocity
as calculated by Newton is found less by one-sixth than
observation gives; and that Laplace sets himself to explain the anomaly. He recognizes the evolution of heat
by the compression which each sound-wave produces in
the air; finds the extra velocity consequent on this;
adds this to the velocity previously calculated; finds the
result answer to the observed fact; and then, having
resolved the phenomenon into its components and
measured them, considers his task concluded. So throughout: the habit is that of identifying, parting, and estimating factors; and stopping after having done this completely.

This habit, carried into the interpretation of things
at large, affects it somewhat as the mathematical habit
affects it. It tends towards the formation of unduly-simple
and unduly-definite conceptions; and it encourages the
natural propensity to be content with proximate results. The daily practice of dealing with single factors of
phenomena, and with factors complicated by but few

others, and with factors ideally separated from their combinations, inevitably gives to the thoughts about surrounding things an analytic rather than a synthetic character. It promotes the contemplation of simple causes apart from the entangled *plexus* of co-operating causes which all the higher natural phenomena show us; and begets a tendency to suppose that when the results of such simple causes have been exactly determined, nothing remains to be asked.

Physical science, then, though indispensable as a means of developing the consciousness of causation in its simple definite forms, and thus preparing the mind for dealing with complex causation, is not sufficient of itself to make complex causation truly comprehensible. In illustration of its inadequacy, I might name a distinguished mathematician and physicist whose achievements place him in the first rank, but who, nevertheless, when entering on questions of concrete science, where the data are no longer few and exact, has repeatedly shown defective judgment. Choosing premises which, to say the least, were gratuitous and in some cases improbable, he has proceeded by exact methods to draw definite conclusions; and has then enunciated those conclusions as though they had a certainty proportionate to the exactness of his methods.

The kind of discipline which affords the needful corrective, is the discipline which the Concrete Sciences give. Study of the *forms* of phenomena, as in Logic and Mathematics, is needful but by no means sufficient. Study of the *factors* of phenomena, as in Mechanics, Physics, Chemistry, is also essential, but not enough by itself, or enough even joined with study of the forms. Study of the *products* themselves, in their totalities, is no less necessary. Exclusive attention to forms and factors not only fails to give right conceptions of products, but even tends to make the conceptions of products wrong. The analytical habit of mind has to be supplemented by the synthetical habit of mind. Seen in its proper place, analysis has for its chief function to prepare the way for synthesis: and to keep a due mental balance, there must be not only a recognition of the truth that synthesis is the end to which analysis is the means, but there must also be a practice of synthesis along with a practice of analysis.

All the Concrete Sciences familiarize the mind with certain cardinal conceptions which the Abstract and Abstract-Concrete Sciences do not yield—the conceptions of *continuity, complexity,* and *contingency.* The simplest of the Concrete Sciences, Astronomy and Geology, yield the idea of continuity with great distinctness. I do not mean continuity of existence merely; I mean continuity of causation: the unceasing production of effect—the never-ending work of every force. On the mind of the astronomer there is vividly impressed the idea that any one planet which has been drawn out of its course by another planet, or by a combination of others, will through all future time follow a route different from that it would have followed but for the perturbation; and he recognizes its reaction upon the perturbing planet or planets, as similarly having effects which, while ever being complicated and ever slowly diffused, will never be lost during the immeasurable periods to come. So, too, the geologist sees in each change wrought on the Earth's crust, by igneous or aqueous action, a new factor that goes on perpetually modifying all subsequent changes. An upheaved portion of seabottom alters the courses of ocean-currents, modifies the climates of adjacent lands, affects their rain-falls and prevailing winds, their denudations and the deposits round their coasts, their floras and faunas; and these effects severally become causes that act unceasingly in ever-multiplying ways. Always there is traceable the persistent working of each force, and the progressive complication of the results through succeeding geologic epochs.

These conceptions, not yielded at all by the Abstract and Abstract-Concrete Sciences, and yielded by the inorganic Concrete Sciences in ways which, though unquestionable, do not arrest attention, are yielded in clear and striking ways by the organic Concrete Sciences—the sciences that deal with living things. Every organism, if we read the lessons it gives, shows us continuity of causation and complexity of causation. The ordinary facts of inheritance illustrate continuity of causation—very conspicuously where varieties so distinct as negro and white are united, and where traces of the negro come out generation after generation; and still better among domestic animals, where traits of remote ancestry show the persistent working of causes which date far back. Organic phenomena make us familiar with complexity of causation, both by showing the co-operation of many antecedents to each consequent, and by showing the multiplicity of results which each influence works out. If we observe how a given weight of a given drug produces on no two persons exactly like effects, and produces even on the same person different effects in different constitutional states; we see at once how involved is the combination of factors by which the changes in an organism are brought about, and how extremely contingent, therefore, is each particular change. And we need but watch what happens after an injury, say of the foot, to perceive how, if permanent, it alters the gait, alters the adjustment and bend of the body, alters the movements of the arms, alters the features into some contracted form accompanying pain or inconvenience. Indeed, through the re-adjustments, muscular, nervous, and visceral, which it entails, this local damage acts and re-acts on function and structure throughout the whole body: producing effects which, as they diffuse, complicate incalculably.

While, in multitudinous ways, the Science of Life thrusts on the attention of the student the cardinal notions of continuity, and complexity, and contingency, of causation, it introduces him to a further conception of moment, which the inorganic Concrete Sciences do not furnish—the conception of what we may call *fructifying* causation. For as it is a distinction between living and not-living bodies that the first propagate while the second do not; it is also a distinction between them that certain actions which go on in the first are cumulative, instead of being, as in the second, dissipative. Not only do organisms as wholes reproduce, and so from small beginnings reach, by multiplication, great results; but components of them, normal and morbid, do the like. Thus a minute portion of a virus introduced into an organism, does not work an effect proportionate to its amount, as would an inorganic agent on an inorganic mass; but by appropriating materials from the blood of the organism, and thus immensely increasing, it works effects altogether out of proportion to its amount as originally introduced—effects which may continue with accumulating power throughout the remaining life of the organism. It is so with internally-evolved agencies as well as with externally-invading agencies. A portion of germinal matter, itself microscopic, may convey from a parent some constitutional peculiarity that is infinitesimal in relation even to its minute bulk; and from this there may arise, fifty years afterwards, gout or insanity in the resulting man: after this great lapse of time, slowly increasing actions and products show themselves in large derangements of function and structure. And this is a trait characteristic of organic phenomena. While from the *destructive* changes going on throughout the tissues of living bodies, there is a continual production of effects which lose themselves by subdivision, as do the effects of inorganic forces; there arise from those *constructive* changes going on in them, by which living bodies are distinguished from not-living bodies, certain classes of effects which increase as they diffuse—go on augmenting in volume as well as in variety.

Thus, as a discipline, study of the Science of Life is essential; partly as familiarizing the mind with the cardinal ideas of continuity, complexity, and contingency, of causation, in clearer and more various ways than do the other Concrete Sciences, and partly as familiarizing the mind with the cardinal idea of fructifying causation, which the other Concrete Sciences do not present at all. Not that, pursued exclusively, the Organic Sciences will yield these conceptions in clear forms: there requires a familiarity with the Abstract-Concrete Sciences to give the requisite grasp of simple causation. Studied by themselves, the Organic Sciences tend rather to make the ideas of causation cloudy; for the reason that the entanglement of the factors and the contingency of the results is so great, that definite relations of antecedents and consequents cannot be established: the two are not presented in such connexions as to make conception of causal action, qualitative and quantitative, sufficiently distinct. There requires, first, the discipline yielded by Physics and Chemistry, to make definite the ideas of forces and actions as necessarily related in their kinds and amounts; and then the study of organic phenomena may be carried on with a clear consciousness that while the processes of causation are so involved as often to be inexplicable, yet there *is* causation, no less necessary and no less exact than causation of simpler kinds.

And now to apply these considerations on mental discipline to our immediate topic. For the effectual study of Sociology there needs a habit of thought generated by the studies of all these sciences—not, of course, an exhaustive, or even a very extensive, study; but such a study as shall give a grasp of the cardinal ideas they severally yield. For, as already said, social phenomena involve phenomena of every order.

That there are necessities of relation such as those with which the Abstract Sciences deal, cannot be denied when it is seen that societies present facts of number and quantity. That the actions of men in society, in all their movements and productive processes, must conform to the laws of the physical forces, is also indisputable. And that everything thought and felt and done in the course of social life, is thought and felt and done in harmony with the laws of individual life, is also a truth—almost a truism, indeed; though one of which few seem conscious.

Scientific culture in general, then, is needful; and above all, culture of the Science of Life. This is more especially requisite, however, because the conceptions of continuity, complexity, and contingency of causation, as well as the conception of fructifying causation, are conceptions common to it and to the Science of Society. It affords a specially-fit discipline, for the reason that it alone among the sciences produces familiarity with these cardinal ideas—presents the data for them in forms easily grasped, and so prepares the mind to recognize the data for them in the Social Science, where they are less easily grasped, though no less constantly presented.

The supreme importance of this last kind of culture, however, is not to be adequately shown by this brief statement. For besides generating habits of thought appropriate to the study of the Social Science, it furnishes special conceptions which serve as keys to the Social Science. The Science of Life yields to the Science of Society, certain great generalizations without which there can be no Science of Society at all.

8. On Poetry*

*Spencer's views on poetry and the classics may be intro-
duced succinctly by reproducing the quotation contained
in the foreword to the edition of his educational essays
published by D. Appleton and Company in 1898. The
quotation from Leslie Stephen reads: "Balston, our
tutor, was a good scholar after the fashion of the day,
and famous for Latin verse; but he was essentially a com-
monplace don. 'Stephen major,' he once said to my
brother, 'if you do not take more pains, how can you ever
expect to write good longs and shorts? If you do not write
good longs and shorts, how can you ever be a man of
taste? If you are not a man of taste, how can you ever
hope to be of use in the world?' " The reader is also asked
to refer to Spencer's views on the same subject in "What
Knowledge Is of Most Worth?"*

Here I may fitly seize the occasion for saying something about my tastes in poetry. A good deal of the feeling which, in a letter to my friend Lott concerning
"Prometheus Unbound," prompted the sentence—"It is
the only poem over which I have ever become enthu-
siastic," was, I believe, due to the fact that it satisfied one
of my organic needs—variety. I say organic, because I
perceive that it runs throughout my constitution, begin-

* *An Autobiography* (New York: D. Appleton and Co., 1904), Vol.
II, pp. 299–302.

ning with likings for food. Monotony of diet is not simply repugnant; it very soon produces indigestion. And an analogous trait seems to pervade my nervous system to its highest ramifications. Both the structure as a whole and all parts of it, soon reach their limits of normal activity, beyond which further activity is alike disagreeable and injurious.

Whether the fact is rightly to be explained thus or not, the fact itself is unquestionable. Even in my boyhood I had a dislike to ballads with recurring burdens; and as I grew older this dislike grew into a disgust which rose almost to exasperation. There was a kind of vicarious shame at this inane repetition of an idea. I recognize, indeed, a few cases in which repetition, when emphasizing a continuously-increasing feeling, is appropriate and very effective; as, for instance, in Tennyson's "Œnone"— "O Mother Ida, hear me ere I die." But usually the repetitions which characterize popular poetry are meaningless, and imply a childish poverty of thought.

Originating, as it seems, in a kindred way, has ever continued an indifference to epic poetry—a want of liking, due in part to the unchanging form of the vehicle and in part to the inadequately varied character of the matter: narratives, incidents, adventures—often of substantially similar kinds. My feeling was well shown when, some twenty years ago, I took up a translation of the *Iliad* for the purpose of studying the superstitions of the early Greeks, and, after reading some six books, felt what a task it would be to go on—felt that I would rather give a large sum than read to the end. Passing over its tedious enumerations of details of dresses and arms, of chariots and horses, of blows given and received, filling page after page—saying nothing of the boyish practice of repeating descriptive names, such as well-greaved Greeks, long-haired Achæans, horse-breaking Trojans, and so forth (epithets which when not relevant to the issue are injurious); passing over, too, the many absurdities, such as giving the genealogy of a horse while in the midst of a battle; and not objecting that the subject-matter appeals continually to brutal passions and the instincts of the savage; it suffices to say that to me the ceaseless repetition of battles and speeches is intolerable. Even did the ideas presented raise pleasurable feelings, a lack of sufficiently broad contrasts in matter and manner would repel me. The like holds with other epic poems—holds, too, when the themes are such as appeal to my sympathies. When reading Dante, for instance, I soon begin to want change in the mode of presentation and change in the quality of the substance, which is too continuously rich: a fabric full of beauties but without beauty in outline—a gorgeous dress ill made up.

Another requirement:—All poetry which I care to read must have intensity. As I have elsewhere said—"While the matter embodied is idealized emotion, the vehicle is the idealized language of emotion"; and, thus regarding emotion as the essence of poetry, it has always seemed to me that an indispensable trait in fine poetry is strong emotion. If the emotion is not of a pronounced kind, the proper vehicle for it is prose; and the rhythmical form becomes proper only as the emotion rises. It is doubtless for this reason that I am in but small measure attracted to Wordsworth. Admitting, though I do, that throughout his works there are sprinkled many poems of great beauty, my feeling is that most of his writing is not wine but beer.

In pursuance of the conception just indicated, I have occasionally argued that the highest type of poetry must be one in which the form continually varies with the matter; rising and falling in its poetical traits according as the wave of emotion grows stronger or becomes weaker —now descending to a prose which has only a suspicion of rhythm in it, and characterized by words and figures of but moderate strength, and now, through various grades, rising to the lyrical form, with its definite measures and vivid metaphors. Attempts have I think been made to produce works having this heterogeneity of form, but with no great success: transcendent genius is required for it.

About others' requirements I cannot of course speak; but my own requirement is—little poetry and of the best. Even the true poets are far too productive. If they would write only one-fourth of the amount, the world would be a gainer. As for the versifiers and the minor poets, they do little more than help to drown good literature in a flood of bad. There is something utterly wearisome in this continual working-up afresh the old materials into slightly different forms—talking continually of skies and stars, of seas and streams, of trees and flowers, sunset and sunrise, the blowing of breezes and the singing of birds, &c.—now describing these familiar things themselves, and now using them in metaphors that are worn threadbare. The poetry commonly produced does not bubble up as a spring but is simply pumped up; and pumped-up poetry is not worth reading.

No one should write verse if he can help it. Let him suppress it if possible; but if it bursts forth in spite of him it may be of value.

9. On Art*

*On one of his few trips abroad, Spencer visited Italy in
1868. The thing that impressed him most was the dead
city of Pompeii. Being a sociologist, he was particularly
interested in "the objects on all sides, and in the marks
of their daily use visible on them." His interest in Rome
was not as great "as that felt by most." But in his autobiography he seized the opportunity to vent his "heresies
concerning the old masters." The excerpt below speaks
clearly for itself.*

In Kugler's *Hand Book of Painting* I read, in the account of Raphael's death:—"Men regarded his works
with religious veneration, as if God had revealed himself through Raphael as in former days through the
prophets." A feeling of this kind relative to Raphael,
widely diffused I suppose, has co-operated with another
feeling, also widely diffused, relative to the old masters
at large. Just as the paper and print forming a Bible
acquire, in most minds, such sacredness that it is an of-
fence to use the volume for any trivial purpose, such as
stopping out a draught; so a picture representing some
Scriptural incident is, in most minds, placed above fault-
finding by its subject. Average people cannot dissociate
the execution from the thing represented; and condem-

* *An Autobiography* (New York: D. Appleton and Co., 1863), Vol.
II, pp. 219–228.

nation of the one implies in their thought disrespect for
the other. By these two feelings, criticism of ancient works
of art has been profoundly vitiated. The judicial faculty
has been mesmerised by the confused halo of piety which
surrounds them.

Hence when, in Kugler, I find it remarked concerning Raphael's "Transfiguration" that "it becomes us to
offer any approach to criticism with all humility"—
when I see the professed critic thus prostrating himself
before a reputation; my scepticism respecting the worth
of the current applause of the old masters is confirmed.
And when those who have "taken exception" to "the two-
fold action contained in this picture" are called by Kugler "shallow critics," I have not the slightest hesitation in
classing myself with them; nor have I the slightest hesitation in rejecting the excuse that this fatal fault "is
explained historically" by the circumstances of the depicted incident. As though a fundamental vice in a work
of art can be got rid of by learning that it is involved in
the scene represented! As though one's eyes, gravitated
now to one, now to the other, of the conflicting centres
of interest, can be prevented from doing so by any such
explanation!

Detailed criticisms cannot be made intelligible when
the painting criticised is not before us; otherwise many
might be passed on "the Transfiguration." For the same
reason it is difficult to deal in any but a general way with
Michael Angelo's frescoes in the Sistine Chapel. Were
they of recent date, we might marvel that the conception
of the Creator is made so little to transcend the conception of the created as in the figures of God and Adam;
and might say that the emergence of Eve out of Adam's
side is effected by a being more like a magician than a
Deity. But when we find the contemporary Protestant

Luther saying in his Table Talk that God "could be rich soon and easily if he would be more provident, and would deny us the use of his creatures," and expressing his belief that "it costeth God yearly more to maintain only the sparrows than the yearly revenue of the French King amounteth unto"—when we find ideas so grossly anthropomorphic in a reformer of the faith, we cannot expect from Michael Angelo, holding the faith in its unreformed state, ideas that are other than grossly anthropomorphic. Passing over criticisms of this class, therefore, and admitting that there are many figures and groups finely drawn (though they exhibit too much his tendency to express mental superiority by supernatural bigness of muscles) let me say something concerning the decorations at large. Here the fault in art is of the same kind as that which is common in the reception-rooms of English houses, where the aim is to achieve two ends that are mutually exclusive—to make a fine whole and to include a crowd of fine parts. Continually one sees saloons so filled with paintings or engravings, statuettes, vases, objects of vertu etc., that they have become little else than picture galleries or cabinets of curiosities; and the general impression is lost in the impressions produced by the multitudinous pretty things. But if a room is to be made itself a work of art, as it should be, then the paintings, statuettes and minor ornaments, must be relatively few in number, must be so distributed that they fall into their places as component parts, and must none of them be obtrusive enough to distract attention from the *ensemble*. The like is true of every interior, no matter what its size or purpose, and, among others, of such an interior as the Sistine Chapel. If this be considered as a receptacle for works of art, then it is faulty because it displays them, or at any rate the greater part of them, in the worst possible ways. If it is considered as in itself a work of art, then it is bad because the effects of its decorative parts conflict too much with the effect of the whole. Its fault as a whole is like the fault of one of its chief components—the fresco of the Last Judgment; over which the eye wanders unable to combine its elements.

Were there anything like discrimination in the praises of pictures by the old masters—were they applauded only for certain merits at the same time that their demerits were recognized, I should have no objection to make. Or were each of them more or less approved as being good relatively to the mental culture of its age, which was characterized by crude ideas and sentiments and undisciplined perceptions, I should agree that many of them deserve praise. But the applause given is *absolute* instead of *relative;* and the grossest absurdities in them are habitually passed over without remark. Take, for example, Guido's much admired fresco, "Phœbus and Aurora." That it has beauty as a composition is undeniable. That the figures of the Hours are gracefully drawn and combined is beyond question. Some of its unobtrusive faults may fitly be forgiven. That the movements of the Hours are such as could not enable them to keep pace with the chariot, and that, being attached to figures which are exposed to "the wind of their own speed," some of the draperies could not assume such forms as are given, are defects which may be passed over; since, when the subject is supernatural, there are traits, such as running on clouds, which are not to be tested by congruity with observable facts. But as utter divergence from the natural in the drawing of the figures, etc. would not have been excused by the supernaturalness of the subject; so, neither should utter divergence from the natural in respect of light and shade be thus excused. In the first place, the country over which the chariot is advancing, instead of being shown as dimly lighted by it, is shown as already in broad daylight—a daylight utterly unaccountable. Far more remarkable than this, however, is the next anomaly. The entire group,—the chariot and horses, the hours and their draperies, and even Phœbus himself,— are represented as illuminated from without: are made visible by some unknown source of light—some other sun! Stranger still is the next thing to be noted. The only source of light indicated in the composition—the torch carried by the flying boy—radiates no light whatever. Not even the face of its bearer, immediately behind, is illumined by it! Nay, this is not all. The crowning absurdity is that the non-luminous flames of this torch are themselves illuminated from elsewhere! The lights and shades by which the forms of the flames are shown, are apparently due to that unknown luminary which lights up the group as a whole, as well as the landscape! Thus we have absurdity piled upon absurdity. And further, we have them in place of the splendid effects which might have been produced had Nature not been gratuitously contradicted. If Phœbus himself had been represented as the faintly-outlined source whence radiated the light upon the horses, the hours, the draperies, the clouds, and the dimly-visible Earth, what a magnificent combination of lights and shades might have been produced: not taking away from, but emphasizing, the beauty of the forms!

"You must not criticize the old masters in this way," I hear said by some. "You must consider the ideas and sentiments expressed by their works, and the skilful composition shown in them, and must overlook these technical defects." Space permitting, I might here ask in how many cases the merits thus assumed exist. But without entering any such demurrer, I will limit myself to the defects classed as technical; and I reply that these are *not* to be overlooked. When it is proved to me that, on reading a poem, I should think only of the fineness of the idea it embodies, and should disregard bad grammar, halting versification, jarring rhymes, cacophonous phrases, mixed metaphors, and so on; then I will admit that in contemplating a picture I may properly ignore the fact that the light is shown to come in various directions or from nowhere in particular. After I have been persuaded that while listening to a piece of music I ought to ignore the false notes, the errors in time, the harshness of *timbre*, as well as the lack of distinction between piano and forte passages, and that I should think only of the feeling which the composer intended to convey; then I will agree that it is proper to pay no regard to the fact that the shades in a picture have been all so unnaturally strengthened as to make them everywhere alike in degree of darkness, (a defect which cannot be explained away as being due to the alleged darkening of the shadows by time). Quite admitting, or rather distinctly affirming, as I do, that truthful representation of the physical aspects of things is an element in pictorial art of inferior rank to the truthful representation of emotion, action, and dramatic combination; I nevertheless contend that the first must be achieved before the second can be duly appreciated. Only when the vehicle is good can that which is to be conveyed be fully brought home to the spectator's consciousness. The first thing to be demanded of a picture is that it shall not shock the perceptions of natural appearances—the cultivated perceptions, I mean. If, as in many works of the old masters, a group of figures standing out of doors is represented with in-door lights and shades upon it; and if a spectator who has looked at

Nature with such careless eyes that he is unconscious of this incongruity, does not have his attention distracted by it from the composition or the sentiment; this fact is nothing to the point. The standard of judgment must be that of the observant—not that of the unobservant. If we may fitly take the verdicts of those who cannot distinguish between truth and untruth in the physioscopy of a picture, we may fitly go further, and make our æsthetic ideas conform to those of the cottager who puts on his mantel-shelf a gaudily painted cast of a parrot, and sticks against his wall a coloured print of the Prodigal Son in blue-coat and yellow breeches.*

In rejoinder to all this, there will doubtless come from many the question—"How about the experts? how happens it that they, who are the most competent judges, applaud these same works of which you speak so disrespectfully?"

My first reply is that, were the truth known, the question would be less unhesitatingly put; for by no means all experts think what they are supposed to think. As there is a religious orthodoxy so is there an æsthetic orthodoxy; and dissent from the last, like dissent from the first, brings on the dissenter the reprobation of the majority,

---

* I venture the new word just used, because there exists no word expressive of *all* those traits in a picture which concerns the physical appearances of the objects represented. Under "physioscopy" I propose to include the rendering of the phenomena of linear perspective, of aeriel perspective, of light and shade, and of colour in so far as it is determined not by artistic choice, but by natural conditions—*e.g.* that of water as affected by the sky, the clouds, and the bottom. The conception, the sentiment, the composition, the expression, may some or all of them be good in a picture of which the physioscopy, in some or all of its elements, is bad; and *vice versa*. The characteristics included in the one group are entirely separate from those included in the other; and there needs a word by which the distinction may be conveyed without circumlocution.

which usually includes all who are in power. Hence it results that many artists—especially when young and
afraid of offending the authorities—refrain from saying
that which they secretly believe respecting traditional
reputations. As I can testify, there are those among them
who do not join in the chorus of applause commonly
given to the painters of past times, but who know that
their æsthetic heterodoxies, if uttered, would make
enemies. When, however, they have reason to think that
what they say will not bring on them the penalties of
heresy, they express opinions quite unlike those they are
assumed to hold.

My second reply is that, so long as the professed approval of artists is unaccompanied by adoption of the
practices of those approved, it goes for little. Imitation
is said to be the sincerest form of flattery—or rather, it
should be, not of flattery, but of admiration; and there
are many traits of the old masters perfectly easy to imitate, which artists would imitate if they really admired
them. Let us again choose illustrations from light and
shade. In the great majority of cases, ancient painters
represented shadows by different gradations of black:
making a tacit assumption like that made by every boy
when he begins to draw. But modern painters do not follow this lead. Though the artist of our day may not have
formed for himself the generalization that a place into
which the direct light cannot fall, being one into which
the indirect and usually diffused, light falls, must have
the average colour of this diffused light (often qualified
by the special lights reflected from particular objects near
at hand), and that therefore a shadow may be of any
colour according to circumstances; yet his empirical
knowledge of this truth makes him studiously avoid the
error which his predecessor commonly fell into. Take

another case. An assumption quite naturally made at the outset, is that surfaces which retreat from the light must in retreating become more deeply shaded; and, in conformity with this assumption, we usually see in old paintings that while the outer parts of shadows are comparatively faint, the parts remote from their edges are made very dark—a contrast which must have existed originally, and cannot have resulted from age. But now-a-days only a tiro habitually does this. The instructed man knows that the interior part of a shadow, often no darker than its exterior part, is, under some conditions, even less dark than the part near its edge; and he rarely finds the conditions such as call upon him to represent the interior part of the shadow by an opaque black. Once more there is the kindred mistake, usual in old paintings, that curved surfaces, as of limbs, where they are shown as turning away from the general light, are habitually not shown as having the limiting parts of their retreating surfaces lighted up by radiations from objects behind; as they in most cases are. But in modern paintings these reflected lights are put in; and a true appearance of roundness is given.

Thus, as I say, in respect of some most conspicuous traits, easily imitated, the artist of our time carefully avoids doing as the ancient artist did; and such being the case, his eulogies, if he utters them, do not go for much. When we have to choose between the evidence derived from words and the evidence derived from deeds, we may fitly prefer the evidence derived from deeds.

10.   On Music*

Of the "creative arts" Spencer paid particular attention to music, which, for him, "in its bearings upon human happiness," was second in importance only to "intellectual language." Music was particularly important in cultivating "the language of emotions." As always, of course, he treated music within the broader doctrine of evolution. Spencer started the essay titled "The Origin and Function of Music" while spending some leisure time at Andarroh, a farmhouse to the north of Dalry, "now in rambling over the moors, now in trying with one or other lure to tempt some salmon which were lying below the falls of the Ken." It first appeared in Fraser's Magazine *October, 1857.*

And now, what is the *function* of music? Has music any effect beyond the immediate pleasure it produces? Analogy suggests that it has. The enjoyments of a good dinner do not end with themselves, but minister to bodily well-being. Though people do not marry with a view to maintain the race, yet the passions which impel them to marry secure its maintenance. Parental affection is a feeling which, while it conduces to parental happiness, ensures the nurture of offspring. Men love to accumulate property, often without thought of the benefits

* *Essays on Education, Etc.* (London: J. M. Dent and Sons, Ltd., 1911), pp. 325–330.

it produces; but in pursuing the pleasure of acquisition they indirectly open the way to other pleasures. The wish for public approval impels all of us to do many things which we should otherwise not do,—to undertake great labours, face great dangers, and habitually rule ourselves in a way that smooths social intercourse: that is, in gratifying our love of approbation we subserve divers ulterior purposes. And, generally, our nature is such that in fulfilling each desire, we in some way facilitate the fulfilment of the rest. But the love of music seems to exist for its own sake. The delights of melody and harmony do not obviously minister to the welfare either of the individual or of society. May we not suspect, however, that this exception is apparent only? Is it not a rational inquiry—What are the indirect benefits which accrue from music, in addition to the direct pleasure it gives?

But that it would take us too far out of our track, we should prelude this inquiry by illustrating at some length a certain general law of progress;—the law that alike in occupations, sciences, arts, the divisions that had a common root, but by continual divergence have become distinct, and are now being separately developed, are not truly independent, but severally act and react on each other to their mutual advancement. Merely hinting thus much, however, by way of showing that there are many analogies to justify us, we go on to express the opinion that there exists a relationship of this kind between music and speech.

All speech is compounded of two elements, the words and the tones in which they are uttered—the signs of ideas and the signs of feelings. While certain articulations express the thought, certain vocal sounds express the more or less of pain or pleasure which the thought gives. Using the word *cadence* in an unusually extended sense, as comprehending all modifications of voice, we may say that *cadence is the commentary of the emotions upon the propositions of the intellect*. The duality of spoken language, though not formally recognised, is recognised in practice by every one; and every one knows that very often more weight attaches to the tones than to the words. Daily experience supplies cases in which the same sentence of disapproval will be understood as meaning little or meaning much, according to the inflections of voice which accompany it; and daily experience supplies still more striking cases in which words and tones are in direct contradiction—the first expressing consent, while the last express reluctance; and the last being believed rather than the first.

These two distinct but interwoven elements of speech have been undergoing a simultaneous development. We know that in the course of civilisation words have been multiplied, new parts of speech have been introduced, sentences have grown more varied and complex; and we may fairly infer that during the same time new modifications of voice have come into use, fresh intervals have been adopted, and cadences have become more elaborate. For while, on the one hand, it is absurd to suppose that, along with the undeveloped verbal forms of barbarism, there existed a developed system of vocal inflections; it is, on the other hand, necessary to suppose that, along with the higher and more numerous verbal forms needed to convey the multiplied and complicated ideas of civilised life, there have grown up those more involved changes of voice which express the feelings proper to such ideas. If intellectual language is a growth, so also, without doubt, is emotional language a growth.

Now, the hypothesis which we have hinted above, is, that beyond the direct pleasure which it gives, music has the indirect effect of developing this language of the emotions. Having its root, as we have endeavoured to show, in those tones, intervals, and cadences of speech which express feeling—arising by the combination and intensifying of these, and coming finally to have an embodiment of its own—music has all along been reacting upon speech, and increasing its power of rendering emotion. The use in recitative and song of inflections more expressive than ordinary ones, must from the beginning have tended to develop the ordinary ones. Familiarity with the more varied combinations of tones that occur in vocal music can scarcely have failed to give greater variety of combination to the tones in which we utter our impressions and desires. The complex musical phrases by which composers have conveyed complex emotions, may rationally be supposed to have influenced us in making those involved cadences of conversation by which we convey our subtler thoughts and feelings.

That the cultivation of music has no effect on the mind, few will be absurd enough to contend. And if it has an effect, what more natural effect is there than this of developing our perception of the meanings of inflections, qualities, and modulations of voice; and giving us a correspondingly increased power of using them? Just as mathematics, taking its start from the phenomena of physics and astronomy, and presently coming to be a separate science, has since reacted on physics and astronomy to their immense advancement—just as chemistry, first arising out of the processes of metallurgy and the industrial arts, and gradually growing into an independent study, has now become an aid to all kinds of production—just as physiology, originating out of medicine and once subordinate to it, but latterly pursued for its own sake, is in our day coming to be the science on which the progress of medicine depends;—so, music, having its root in emotional language, and gradually evolved from it, has ever been reacting upon and further advancing it. Whoever will examine the facts will find this hypothesis to be in harmony with the method of civilisation everywhere displayed.

It will scarcely be expected that much direct evidence in support of this conclusion can be given. The facts are of a kind which it is difficult to measure, and of which we have no records. Some suggestive traits, however, may be noted. May we not say, for instance, that the Italians, among whom modern music was earliest cultivated, and who have more especially practised and excelled in melody (the division of music with which our argument is chiefly concerned)—may we not say that these Italians speak in more varied and expressive inflections and cadences than any other nation? On the other hand, may we not say that, confined almost exclusively as they have hitherto been to their national airs, which have a marked family likeness, and therefore accustomed to but a limited range of musical expression, the Scotch are unusually monotonous in the intervals and modulations of their speech? And again, do we not find among different classes of the same nation, differences that have like implications? The gentleman and the clown stand in a very decided contrast with respect to variety of intonation. Listen to the conversation of a servant-girl, and then to that of a refined, accomplished lady, and the more delicate and complex changes of voice used by the latter will be conspicuous. Now, without going so far as to say that out of all the differences of culture to which the upper and lower classes are subjected, difference of musical culture is that to which alone this difference of speech is ascribable, yet we may fairly say that there seems a much more obvious connection of cause and effect between these than between any others. Thus, while the inductive evidence to which we can appeal is but scanty and vague, yet what there is favours our position.

Probably most will think that the function here assigned to music is one of very little moment. But further reflection may lead them to a contrary conviction. In its bearings upon human happiness, we believe that this emotional language which musical culture develops and refines is only second in importance to the language of the intellect; perhaps not even second to it. For these modifications of voice produced by feelings are the means of exciting like feelings in others. Joined with gestures and expressions of face, they give life to the otherwise dead words in which the intellect utters its ideas; and so enable the hearer not only to *understand* the state of mind they accompany, but to *partake* of that state. In short, they are the chief media of *sympathy*. And if we consider how much both our general welfare and our immediate pleasures depend upon sympathy, we shall recognise the importance of whatever makes this sympathy greater. If we bear in mind that by their fellow-feeling men are led to behave justly, kindly, and considerately to each other—that the difference between the cruelty of the barbarous and the humanity of the civilised, results from the increase of fellow-feeling; if we bear in mind that this faculty which makes us sharers in the joys and sorrows of others, is the basis of all the higher affections—that in friendship, love, and all domestic pleasures, it is an essential element; if we bear in mind how much our direct gratifications are intensified by sympathy,—how, at the theatre, the concert, the picture gallery, we lose half our enjoyment if we have no one to enjoy with us; if, in short, we bear in mind that for all happiness beyond what the unfriended recluse can have, we are indebted to this same sympathy;—we shall see that the agencies which communicate it can scarcely be overrated in value.

The tendency of civilisation is more and more to repress the antagonistic elements of our characters and to develop the social ones—to curb our purely selfish desires and exercise our unselfish ones—to replace private gratifications by gratifications resulting from, or involving, the happiness of others. And while, by this adaptation to the social state, the sympathetic side of our nature is being unfolded, there is simultaneously growing up a language of sympathetic intercourse—a language through which we communicate to others the happiness we feel, and are made sharers in their happiness.

This double process, of which the effects are already sufficiently appreciable, must go on to an extent of which we can as yet have no adequate conception. The habitual concealment of our feelings diminishing, as it must, in proportion as our feelings become such as do not demand concealment, we may conclude that the exhibition of them will become much more vivid than we now dare allow it to be; and this implies a more expressive emotional language. At the same time, feelings of a higher and more complex kind, as yet experienced only by the cultivated few, will become general; and there will be a corresponding development of the emotional language into more involved forms. Just as there has silently grown up a language of ideas, which, rude as it at first was, now enables us to convey with precision the most subtle and complicated thoughts; so, there is still silently growing up a language of feelings, which, notwithstanding its present imperfection, we may expect will ultimately enable men vividly and completely to impress on each other all the emotions which they experience from moment to moment.

Thus if, as we have endeavoured to show, it is the function of music to facilitate the development of this emotional language, we may regard music as an aid to the achievement of that higher happiness which it indistinctly shadows forth. Those vague feelings of unexperienced felicity which music arouses—those indefinite impressions of an unknown ideal life which it calls up, may be considered as a prophecy, to the fulfilment of which music is itself partly instrumental. The strange capacity which we have for being so affected by melody and harmony may be taken to imply both that it is within the possibilities of our nature to realise those intenser delights they dimly suggest, and that they are in some way concerned in the realisation of them. On this supposition the power and the meaning of music become comprehensible; but otherwise they are a mystery.

We will only add, that if the probability of these corollaries be admitted, then music must take rank as the highest of the fine arts—as the one which, more than any other, ministers to human welfare. And thus, even leaving out of view the immediate gratifications it is hourly giving, we cannot too much applaud that progress of musical culture which is becoming one of the characteristics of our age.

11.   On Culture*

Culture was a concept frequently discussed in nineteenth century educational writings. Spencer used the term culture in at least two senses: as "knowledge" and as "cultivation" or "training." He often talked about several types of culture, e.g., intellectual, scientific, literary, religious, aesthetic, physical, etc., as shown in his educational essays previously cited and as can be seen in the excerpt below. In this latter one, which forms a chapter of his The Principles of Ethics *(1892), Spencer, for the most part, argues in a vein similar to that in his previous writings, but one notices also some interesting slight variations. In addition to re-emphasizing the moral and ethical aspects of "scientific culture," his position on the value of historical knowledge and literary and aesthetic culture is more mellow than in "What Knowledge Is of Most Worth?" He recognized, for example, that a certain attention to the "personal elements" of history is valuable. And, if we may be allowed to use an Aristotelian metaphor, he called for a "golden mean" in education. In connection with his views expressed in his treatise on ethics, Spencer wrote: ". . . to achieve the fullest life and greatest happiness, a due proportion must be maintained among the activities of the various faculties; excess in one and deficiency in another being, by implication, negatived."†*

---

* *The Principles of Ethics* (New York and London: D. Appleton and Co., 1892), Vol. I, pp. 514–522. This was the last volume in the synthetic philosophy series.

† *Life and Letters*, II, 364.

219. Taken in its widest sense, culture means preparation for complete living. It includes, in the first place, all such discipline and all such knowledge as are needful for, or conducive to, efficient self-sustentation and sustentation of family. And it includes, in the second place, all such development of the faculties at large, as fits them for utilizing those various sources of pleasure which Nature and Humanity supply to responsive minds.

The first of these two divisions of culture has more than an ethical sanction: it is ethically enjoined. Acquisition of fitness for carrying on the business of life is primarily a duty to self and secondarily a duty to others. If under the head of this fitness we comprise, as we must, such skill as is needful for those who are to be manually occupied, as well as skill of every higher kind, it becomes manifest that (save with those who have sustentation *gratis*) lack of it makes a healthy physical life impracticable, and makes impracticable the nurture of dependents. Further, the neglect to acquire a power of adequately maintaining self and offspring, necessitates either the burdening of others in furnishing aid, or else, if they refuse to do this, necessitates that infliction of pain upon them which the contemplation of misery causes.

Concerning the second division of culture, peremptory obligation is not to be alleged. Those who take an ascetic view of life have no reason for that discipline of faculties which aims to increase one or other refined pleasure; and, as among the Quakers, we see that there does in fact result a disregard of, and often a reprobation of, such discipline, or of parts of it. Only those who accept hedonism can consistently advocate this exercise of intellect and feeling which prepares the way for various gratifications filling leisure hours. They only can regard it as needful for attaining complete life, and as therefore having an ethical sanction.

From these general ideas of culture, essential and non-essential, let us go on to consider the several divisions of it.

220. There is a part of culture, usually neglected, which should be recognized alike by those to whom it brings means of living and by those who do not seek material profit from it, which may fitly stand first. I mean the acquirement of manual dexterity.

That this is a proper preparation for life among those occupied in productive industry, will not be disputed; though at present, even the boys who may need it are but little encouraged to acquire manipulative skill: only those kinds of skill which games give are cultivated. But manipulative skill and keenness of perception ought to be acquired by those also who are to have careers of higher kinds. Awkwardness of limb and inability to use the fingers deftly, continually entail small disasters and occasionally great ones; while expertness frequently comes in aid of welfare, either of self or others. One who has been well practised in the uses of his senses and his muscles, is less likely than the unpractised to meet with accidents; and, when accidents occur, is sure to be more efficient in rectifying mischiefs. Were it not that this obvious truth is ignored, it would be absurd to point out that, since limbs and senses exist to the end of adjusting the actions to surrounding objects and movements, it is the business of every one to gain skill in the performance of such actions.

Let it not be supposed that I am here advocating the extension of *formal* culture in this direction: very much to the contrary. The shaping of all education into lessons is one of the vices of the time. Cultivation of manipulative skill, in common with expertness in general, should be acquired in the process of achieving ends otherwise desired. In any rationally-conducted education there must be countless occasions for the exercise of those faculties which the artisan and the experimenter bring perpetually into play.

221. Intellectual culture under its primary aspect links on to the culture just described; for as discipline of the limbs and senses is a fitting of them for direct dealings with things around, so intelligence, in its successive grades, is an agent for guiding dealings of indirect kinds, greater and greater in their complexity. The higher acquisitions and achievements of intellect have now become so remote from practical life, that their relations to it are usually lost sight of. But if we remember that in the stick employed to heave up a stone, or the paddle to propel a boat, we have illustrations of the uses of levers; while in the pointing of an arrow so as to allow for its fall during flight, certain dynamical principles are tacitly recognized; and that from these vague early cognitions the progress may be traced step by step to the generalizations of mathematicians and astronomers; we see that science has gradually emerged from the crude knowledge of the savage. And if we remember that as this crude knowledge of the savage served for simple guidance of his life-sustaining actions, so the developed sciences of mathematics and astronomy serve for guidance in the workshop and the counting-house and for steering of vessels, while developed physics and chemistry preside over all manufacturing processes; we see that at the one extreme as at the other, furtherance of men's ability to deal effectually with the surrounding world, and so to satisfy their wants, is that purpose of intellectual culture which precedes all others.

Even for these purposes we distinguish as practical, that intellectual culture which makes us acquainted with the natures of things, should be wider than is commonly thought needful. Preparation for this or that kind of business is far too special. There cannot be adequate knowledge of a particular class of natural facts without some knowledge of other classes. Every object and every action simultaneously presents various orders of phenomena—mathematical, physical, chemical,—with, in many cases, others which are vital; and these phenomena are so interwoven that full comprehension of any group involves partial comprehension of the rest. Though at first sight the extent of intellectual culture thus suggested as requisite may seem impracticable, it is not so. When education is rightly carried on, the cardinal truths of each science may be clearly communicated and firmly grasped, apart from the many corollaries commonly taught along with them. And after there has been gained such familiarity with these cardinal truths of the several sciences as renders their chief implications comprehensible, it becomes possible to reach rational conceptions of any one group of phenomena, and to be fully prepared for a special occupation.

That division of intellectual culture which comprises knowledge of the sciences, while having an indirect ethical sanction as conducing to self-sustentation and sustentation of others, has also a direct sanction irrespective of practical ends. To the servant-girl, the ploughboy, the grocer, nay even to the average classical scholar or man of letters, the world, living and dead, with the universe around it, present no such grand panorama as they do to those who have gained some conception of the actions, infinite and infinitesimal, everywhere going on, and can contemplate them under other aspects than the technical. If we imagine that into a gorgeously-decorated hall a rush-light is brought, and, being held near to some part of the wall, makes visible the pattern over a small area of it, while everything else remains in darkness; and if, instead of this, we imagine that electric lights turned on reveal simultaneously the whole room with its varied contents; we may form some idea of the different appearance under which Nature is contemplated by the utterly uncultured mind and by the highly cultured mind. Whoever duly appreciates this immense contrast will see that, rightly assimilated, science brings exaltation of mental life.

One further result must be recognized. That study of all orders of phenomena which, while it gives adequate general conceptions of them, leads, now in this direction and now in that, to limits which no exploration can transcend, is needful to make us aware of our relation to the ultimate mystery of things; and so to awaken a consciousness which we may properly consider germane to the ethical consciousness.

222. In its full acceptation, knowledge of science includes knowledge of social science; and this includes a certain kind of historical knowledge. Such of it as is needful for political guidance, each citizen should endeavour to obtain. Though the greater parts of the facts from which true sociological generalizations may be drawn, are presented only by those savage and semi-civilized societies ignored in our educational courses, there are also required some of the facts furnished by the histories of developed nations.

But beyond the impersonal elements of history which chiefly demand attention, a certain attention may rightly be given to its personal elements. Commonly these occupy the entire attention. The great-man-theory of history, tacitly held by the ignorant in all ages and in recent times definitely enunciated by Mr. Carlyle, implies that knowledge of history is constituted by knowledge of rulers and their doings; and by this theory there is fostered in the mass of minds a love of gossip about dead individuals, not much more respectable than the love of gossip about individuals now living. But while no information concerning kings and popes, and ministers and generals, even when joined to exhaustive acquaintance with intrigues and treaties, battles and sieges, gives any insight into the laws of social evolution—while the single fact that division of labour has been progressing in all advancing nations regardless of the will of law-makers, and unobserved by them, suffices to show that the forces which mould societies work out their results apart from, and often in spite of, the aims of leading men; yet a certain moderate number of leading men and their actions may properly be contemplated. The past stages in human progress, which every one should know something about, would be conceived in too shadowy a form if wholly divested of ideas of the persons and events associated with them. Moreover, some amount of such knowledge is requisite to enlarge adequately the conception of human nature in general—to show the extremes, occasionally good but mostly bad, which it is capable of reaching.

With culture of this kind there naturally goes purely literary culture. That a fair amount of this should be included in the preparation for complete living, needs no saying. Rather does it need saying that in a duly proportioned education, as well as in adult life, literature should be assigned less space than it now has. Nearly all are prone to mental occupations of easy kinds, or kinds which yield pleasurable excitements with small efforts; and history, biography, fiction, poetry, are, in this respect, more attractive to the majority than science—more attractive than that knowledge of the order of things at large which serves for guidance.

Still, we must not here forget that from the hedonistic point of view, taking account of this pleasure directly obtained, literary culture has a high claim; and we may also admit that, as conducing to wealth and force of expression by furnishing materials for metaphor and allusion, it increases mental power and social effectiveness. In the absence of it conversation is bald.

223. In culture, as in other things, men tend towards one or other extreme. Either, as with the great majority, culture is scarcely pursued at all, or, as with the few, it is pursued almost exclusively, and often with disastrous results.

Emerson says of the gentleman that the first requisite is to be a good animal, and this is the first requisite for every one. A course of life which sacrifices the animal, though it may be defensible under special conditions is not defensible as a general policy. Within the sphere of our positive knowledge we nowhere see mind without life; we nowhere see life without a body; we nowhere see a full life—a life which is high alike in respect of intensity, breadth, and length—without a healthy body. Every breach of the laws of bodily health produces a physical damage, which eventually damages in some way, though often in an invisible way, the mental health.

Culture has therefore to be carried on subject to other needs. Its amount must be such as consists with, and is conducive to, physical welfare; and it must be also such as consists with, and is conducive to, normal activity not only of the mental powers exercised, but of all others. When carried to an extent which diminishes vivacity, and produces indifference to the various natural enjoyments, it is an abuse; and still more is it an abuse when, as often happens, it is pushed so far as to produce digust with the subjects over which attention has been unduly strained.

Especially in the case of women is condemnation of overculture called for, since immense mischief is done by it. We are told that the higher education, as now carried on at Girton and Newnham, is not inconsistent with maintenance of good health; and if we omit those who are obliged to desist, this appears to be true. I say advisedly "appears to be true." There are various degrees of what is called good health. Commonly it is alleged and admitted where no physical disturbance is manifest; but there is a wide space between this and that full health which shows itself in high spirits and overflowing energy. In women, especially, there may be maintained a health which seems good, and yet falls short of the requirements of the race. For in women, much more than in men, there is constitutionally provided a surplus vitality devoted to continuance of the species. When the system is overtaxed the portion thus set aside is considerably diminished before the portion which goes to carry on individual life is manifestly trenched upon. The cost of activity, and especially of cerebral activity, which is very costly, has to be met; and if expenditure is excessive it cannot be met without deduction from that reserve power which should go to race-maintenance. The reproductive capacity is diminished in various degrees—sometimes to the extent of inability to bear children, more frequently to the extent of inability to yield milk, and in numerous cases to a smaller extent which I must leave unspecified. I have good authority for saying that one of the remoter results of over-culture, very frequently becomes a cause of domestic alienation.

Let me add that an adequately high culture, alike of men and women, might be compassed without mischief were our *curriculum* more rational. If the worthless knowledge included in what is now supposed to be a good education were omitted, all that which is needful for guidance, most of that which is desirable for general enlightenment, and a good deal of that which is distinguished as decorative, might be acquired without injurious reactions.

224. To the egoistic motives for culture have to be added the altruistic motives. A human being devoid of knowledge, and with none of that intellectual life which discipline of the faculties gives, is utterly uninteresting. To become a pleasure-yielding person is a social duty. Hence culture, and especially the culture which conduces to enlivenment, has an ethical sanction and something more.

Especially is this true of æsthetic culture, of which no note has thus far been taken. While it is to be enjoined as aiding that highest development of self required for the fullest life and happiness, it is also to be enjoined as increasing the ability to gratify those around. Though practices in the plastic arts, in music, and in poetry, are usually to be encouraged chiefly as producing susceptibility to pleasures, which the æsthetically uncultured cannot have; yet those who are endowed with something more than average ability, should be led to develop it by motives of benevolence also. In the highest degree this is so with music; and concerted music, subordinating as it does the personal element, is above all other kinds to be cultivated on altruistic grounds. It should be added, however, that excess of æsthetic culture, in common with excess of intellectual culture, is to be reprobated; not in this case because of the over-tax entailed, but because of the undue expenditure of time—the occupation of too large a space in life. With multitudes of people, especially women, the pursuit of beauty in one or other form is the predominant pursuit. To the achievement of prettiness much more important ends are sacrificed. Though æsthetic culture has to be recognized as ethically sanctioned, yet instead of emphasizing the demand for it, there is far greater occasion for condemning the excess of it. There needs a trenchant essay on æsthetic vices, which are everywhere shown in the subordination of use to appearance.

ANDREAS M. KAZAMIAS, Professor of Educational Policy Studies at the University of Wisconsin, was born in Cyprus in 1927. He received his B.A. from the University of Bristol, his S.M. from Fort Hays State College (Kansas), and his Ed.D. from Harvard University. Before joining the University of Wisconsin faculty in 1965, Professor Kazamias taught in the secondary schools of Cyprus and at Oberlin College and the University of Chicago. His writings include *Politics, Society and Secondary Education in England* (1966) and *Education and the Quest for Modernity in Turkey* (1966). He is the co-author of *Tradition and Change in Education: A Comparative Study* (1965) and co-editor of *The Educated Man: Studies in the History of Educational Thought* (1965).